Behaviorism, Neobehaviorism, and Cognitivism in Learning Theory:

Historical and Contemporary Perspectives

JOHN M. MacEACHRAN MEMORIAL LECTURE SERIES

The Department of Psychology at the University of Alberta inaugurated the MacEachran Memorial Lecture Series in 1975 in honor of the late Professor John M. MacEachran. Professor MacEachran was born in Ontario in 1877 and received a Ph.D. in Philosophy from Queen's University in 1905. In 1906 he left for Germany to begin more formal study in psychology, first spending just less than a year in Berlin with Stumpf, and then moving to Leipzig, where he completed a second Ph.D. in 1908 with Wundt as his supervisor. During this period he also spent time in Paris studying under Durkheim and Henri Bergson. With these impressive qualifications the University of Alberta was particularly fortunate in attracting him to its faculty in 1909.

Professor MacEachran's impact has been significant at the university, provincial, and national levels. At the University of Alberta he offered the first courses in psychology and subsequently served as Head of the Department of Philosophy and Psychology and Provost of the University until his retirement in 1945. It was largely owing to his activities and example that several areas of academic study were established on a firm and enduring basis. In addition to playing a major role in establishing the Faculties of Medicine, Education and Law in this Province, Professor MacEachran was also instrumental in the formative stages of the Mental Health Movement in Alberta. At a national level, he was one of the founders of the Canadian Psychological Association and also became its first Honorary President in 1939. John M. MacEachran was indeed one of the pioneers in the development of psychology in Canada.

Perhaps the most significant aspect of the MacEachran Memorial Lecture Series has been the continuing agreement that the Department of Psychology at the University of Alberta has with Lawrence Erlbaum Associates, Publishers, Inc., for the publication of each lecture series. The following is a list of the Invited Speakers and the titles of their published lectures:

1975   Frank A. Geldard (Princeton University)
"Sensory Saltation: Metastability in the Perceptual World"

1976   Benton J. Underwood (Northwestern University)
"Temporal Codes for Memories: Issues and Problems"

1977   David Elkind (Rochester University)
"The Child's Reality: Three Developmental Themes"

1978   Harold Kelley (University of California at Los Angeles)
        "Personal Relationships: Their Structures and Processes"

1979   Robert Rescorla (Yale University)
        "Pavlovian Second-Order Conditioning:
        Studies in Associative Learning"

1980   Mortimer Mishkin (NIMH-Bethesda)
        "Cognitive Circuits" (*unpublished*)

1981   James Greeno (University of Pittsburgh)
        "Current Cognitive Theory in Problem Solving" (*unpublished*)

1982   William Uttal (University of Michigan)
        "Visual Form Detection in 3-Dimensional Space"

1983   Jean Mandler (University of California at San Diego)
        "Stories, Scripts, and Scenes: Aspects of Schema Theory"

1984   George Collier and Carolyn Rovee-Collier
          (Rutgers University)
        "Learning and Motivation: Function and
        Mechanism" (*unpublished*)

1985   Alice Eagly (Purdue University)
        "Sex Differences in Social Behavior:
        A Social-Role Interpretation"

1986   Karl Pribram (Stanford University)
        "Brain Organization in Perception:
        Holonomy and Structure in Figural
        Processing" (*in press*)

1987   Abram Amsel (University of Texas at Austin)
        "Behaviorism, Neobehaviorism, and Cognitivism
        in Learning Theory: Historical and Contemporary
        Perspectives"

                        Eugene C. Lechelt, Coordinator
                        MacEachran Memorial Lecture Series

Sponsored by The Department of Psychology, The University of Alberta with the support of The Alberta Heritage Foundation for Medical Research in memory of John M. MacEachran, pioneer in Canadian psychology.

Behaviorism, Neobehaviorism, and Cognitivism in Learning Theory:

Historical and Contemporary Perspectives

Abram Amsel

University of Texas at Austin

LEA LAWRENCE ERLBAUM ASSOCIATES, PUBLISHERS
1989 Hillsdale, New Jersey   Hove and London

Lawrence Erlbaum Associates, Inc., Publishers
365 Broadway
Hillsdale, New Jersey 07642

Library of Congress Cataloging in Publication Data
Amsel, Abram.
    Behaviorism, neobehaviorism, and cognitivism in learning theory:
historical and contemporary perspectives   by Abram Amsel.
        p.   cm. — (MacEachran memorial lecture series)
    Includes index.
    ISBN 0-8058-0332-7
    1. Learning, Theory of. 2. Behaviorism (psychology). 3. Cognitive
psychology. 4. Learning, Theory of—History. 5. Behaviorism
(Psychology)—History. 6. Cognitive psychology—History.
I. Title. II. Series: John M. MacEachran memorial lecture series.
BF318.A47 1988
153.1′5—dc19   88-11278
                                                     CIP

Printed in the United States of America
10 9 8 7 6 5 4 3 2

To

Tess

and

To the memory of

Annie and Aaron (Harry) Amsel

Contents

Preface

I was undecided about what to present in The MacEachran Lectures, on which this slim volume is based, for I had in mind two quite different things. One was a review of my own theoretical and experimental work. (In psychology, unlike in physics, theory and experiments usually reside in a single investigator.) The second possible subject I saw stemmed from my dissatisfaction, not to say unhappiness, with the current state of affairs in the field of learning theory—specifically in learning theory involving animals—that followed the so-called "cognitive revolution" in psychology. I concluded that I would never have a better forum in which, or a better platform from which, I might express my views on this second subject, so I decided to proceed with the latter, more polemical alternative.

I want to make clear at the beginning how I would characterize this essay. Though not a philosopher, I will be venturing into a realm of discourse that is known as philosophy of science; and though not a historian, I will be dabbling in the history of psychology, unabetted by the scholarly sweep of more distant historical perspective. I would, then, characterize the lectures as criticism—and a one-man's-opinion kind of criticism at that. My credentials for being thus engaged are no more impressive—though no less, either—than those of most who have spent close to four decades rather continuously in the study of conditioning and learning. There are those who would say that during these years my theoretical outlook has not changed very much, that I have been intermittently frustrated and consequently persistent, just as my theorizing requires. Perhaps, in the end, this persistence is the chief credential I bring to this particular work.

I would like to register just one more caveat, and this one can be stated most precisely in terms employed some years ago by Rozeboom (1970) in a paper on the "metascience" of psychological theory. He identified "two formal dimensions along which discussions of psychological theory can vary" (p. 55). One he called *level of abstraction* or *substantivity of concern*; the other he called *acuity* or *penetration*. My caveat is stated in relation to both of these dimensions.

The level-of-abstraction dimension ranges from attention to "specific extant theories . . . at one extreme, . . . [to] philosophy-of-science type concerns for the nature of functioning of idealized theories in general, detached from any real-life instances, at the other" (p. 55). I would characterize this essay as high in *substantivity of concern* and low in *level of abstraction*, in Rozeboom's sense: I am not dealing here with "idealized theories."

According to Rozeboom, metatheoretical acuity

> concerns the degree to which the discussion makes a serious, intellectually responsible attempt to further our understanding of the matter with which it deals. Here the possibilities range from painstaking attention to technical details, to loose and largely gratuitous generalities built around everyday intuitions, or poorly defined neologisms whose literal relevance to anything in reality is tenuous or nonexistent. Unfortunately, disciplined thinking *about* science appears to be much more difficult to achieve than disciplined thinking within it, with the result that to date, very little metascience has managed to get far from the casual, dilettante or intuitional end of the acuity scale, especially at the higher levels of abstraction. (pp. 55–56)

I will compromise with my own doubts on this one, and characterize the metatheoretical level of acuity of my argument as lying somewhere around the middle of the acuity dimension.

In important respects, this book can be seen as an extension and elaboration of a retrospective review I was asked to write of Watson's famous book, *Psychology from the Standpoint of a Behaviorist* (1919), which appeared in *Contemporary Psychology* in 1982. While rereading this book, probably for the first time since my graduate-student days, I was struck by the difference between what I have called Watson's 1913/1919 stance and his later more hardened behaviorism. Also, I noticed the similarity of this sequence and Skinner's theoretical stances in 1938 and in 1950, and what I saw so clearly to be the compatibility between Watson's early views and those of the neobehaviorists, particularly Tolman and Hull. The basic differences I saw between the cognitive behaviorism of Tolman and the cognitivism in current animal learning research was the "fact" that completed for me the thematic structure of this book.

Part of Chapter 3 is taken, in revised form, from the Daniel E. Berlyne Memorial Lecture delivered at the University of Toronto in March, 1986 (published as Amsel, 1986), and from the I. E. Farber Leture on Theory in Psychology delivered in Chicago in May, 1986.

The chapters are presented in a form that is very close to their lecture form, and the colloquial style of, and the personal allusions in, portions of the written version reflects this fact—as does the excessive occurrence of the first-person singular and examples drawn from my own publications. The reader will, I hope, forgive me for this: It is simply much easier to find such examples.

The usual Preface frequently includes an acknowledgment of helpful criticisms and suggestions offered by a number of readers of the manuscript—and then goes on to absolve these people of any responsibility for any errors or wrong-headedness that is still contained in the published work. At the stage where I might have sought the advice and expertise of such persons, I decided against it. This is an "opinion piece," a sort of long editorial. Knowing that I would stubbornly resist attempts to set me straight (and because this might be my only opportunity or inclination to write a piece of polemics of this size), I opted to shield potential advance readers from any guilt by association they might suffer despite the usual—and sometimes suspect—disclaimers.

The first draft of this material was completed while I was a Fellow at the Center for Advanced Study in the Behavioral Sciences, in Stanford, California. For financial support of my Fellowship at the Center under Grant BNS 84-11738, I am grateful to the National Science Foundation. I am indebted to the Center for providing a quiet and congenial interlude in my professional life in which this work could be done, and for the excellent support of the members of its word-processing staff, under the able supervision of Kay Holm. Subsequent drafts were processed at the University of Texas with dedication, skill, and precision by Sandra Foster. My wife, Tess, performed a critical reading of the entire manuscript to make sure the words, the syntax, and the tenses were right.

The invitation to deliver the MacEachran Lectures at the University of Alberta in November of 1987 provided the impetus for writing this little book and the mechanism for its publication. I am grateful to all those who had a part in this invitation, in particular Vincent DiLollo, and to him and to his colleagues in the Psychology Department for their warm hospitality during my stay in Edmonton.

Abram Amsel

1

Setting the Stage:
Behaviorisms and Cognitivisms

I have on occasion used a parliamentary metaphor to characterize the confrontation over the years between those who have taken a stimulus-response (S-R) behavioristic approach and those who favor a cognitive approach in their theorizing about behavior— and I like to point out that the S-R psychologists, who at one time formed the government, are now in the loyal opposition, the cognitivists being the new government. As we shall also see, however, the older generation of cognitivists, who were for the most part the followers of Tolman, were also neobehaviorists; the recent ones are cognitivists in a much more polarized sense—and *they* are the present government.

A parliamentary government, by virtue of its leadership and responsibility, is constantly on the defensive, and this was certainly the case in the days of S-R leadership. The wake of the "cognitive revolution" swept into power even those for whom invertebrates are taken to be cognitive. Unaccountably, however, the posture of the S-R neobehavioristic leadership, which now found itself in opposition, did not change: By failing to *act* like an opposition and to put the cognitivists on the defensive, we found ourselves still on the defensive. It has taken us a long time to change our habits—

to take the offensive role and posture. As I will point out, there have been a couple of recent moves in this direction, one by a behaviorist, Dinsmoor, the other by a neobehaviorist, Denny. I have taken this occasion to add my voice to this movement against the cognitive government, and particularly the animal-cognitivist branch of this government, and to take my place in the opposition side.

I will be referring to cognitive psychology and particularly "animal cognition" as they relate to behavior theory (and particularly learning theory), and I am willing to confess that the cognitive revolution that has occurred in psychology, and particularly in the psychology of animal learning, has left my theoretical style largely unaffected. Although, as has been pointed out to me many times, I work with and theorize about mechanisms emphasizing mediation and anticipation, that can obviously be characterized as cognitive, my empirical constructs are still clothed in the stimulus-response language associated with behaviorism. I find this approach at the same time more analytical and more constraining than the more mentalistic cognitive approach, and I think a little constraint goes a long way in theorizing about behavior and its determinants. My hope is that you may even find some virtue in this more constraining approach to theory that I favor.

The outline of this book is approximately as follows and it proceeds from a broad to a specific domain:

1. I will discuss very briefly experimental psychology—what it was and what it seems to have become.

2. I will discuss briefly and in general terms the recent cognitive revolution in experimental psychology specifically in relation to its attacks on behaviorism.

3. I will then develop in greater detail my position on a subject that I am better qualified to discuss: the cognitive revolution as it has affected learning theory, particularly that part of learning theory—the major part—that has always been based on the study of animals as subjects.

Let me expand a bit on this last assertion (and I will do so even more later). The experimental origins of learning theory were in the work of Thorndike and Pavlov; and its theoretical heyday in America was in the formulations of Guthrie, Hull, Skinner and Tolman, and their followers. Their work was based almost entirely on animal experiments. This tradition, with the very few exceptions in the work of Thorndike and Hull, was distinct from the experimental study of human memory, that originated in the "experimental" work of Ebbinghaus (on himself as subject), and was not at first strongly theoretical.

I have always considered that learning theory, a branch of functionalism, based as it was almost exclusively on animal experimentation, provided the mechanisms for the non-intentional aspects of habit formation, for the acquisition through simple conditioning and learning of the emotional, temperamental, dispositional and attitudinal states and processes—the kind of learning-without-awareness that, collectively, make up part of what we call personality. This essential feature of learning theory is evident in at least portions of the work of Guthrie, Tolman, and Hull, and is particularly clear in certain of Hull's intellectual descendants, such as N. E. Miller and O. H. Mowrer—and in my own work. It is also, but to a lesser extent, the thrust of Skinner's work, which can be regarded as a major contribution to our understanding of skilled (patterned and timed) behavior because of its attention to the intricacies of the reinforcement of response patterns and temporal sequences.

Nonetheless, Skinner's conception of shaping behavior through reinforcement of operants is an essential feature of non-intentionality. It is perhaps not so remarkable that theories which account for this level of learning and behavior should have been studied almost entirely in animals: in dogs, cats, rats, and pigeons, and to a lesser extent (and more recently) in other animals—rabbits, monkeys. I will come back to this point in the next chapter.

The experimental study of memory (or "human learning," as it was called) was also a branch of functionalism, and was pursued originally by associationists, using as subjects college sophomores. It often involved the use of lists and pairs of words or nonsense syllables, and its theoretical language—proactive and retroactive inhibition, intraserial interference—stayed very close to its methods. In the nearer term the study of memory has become structuralist. It has been a major topic for a variety of cognitive psychologists, who have changed and expanded the experimental material to correspond to their changing interests. Still, there is little if anything in this tradition, even in its newer forms, that deals with the dispositional, emotional–motivational, or the temperamental aspects of behavior. The object of study is, with rare exception, still the adult human, and the interest still not so much with acquisition processes as with memory: retention, recall, and recognition. However the newer studies of memory are more theoretical, dealing with the "structures" of short-term and long-term memory, often in the language of information processing. But the point is that however memory was studied, it could be described as an activity that was intentional on the part of the subject, and so the term "cognition" seemed to be more apt in its explanations.

More recently, with the rise of interest in studying the pathology of memory—such as in Korsakoff's and Alzheimer's syndromes and attentional disorders in children (and infantile amnesia in animals)—experimental studies of memory have often turned to animal models, and the fields of learning and memory have begun to come together, to the extent at least that they have often employed similar or comparable experimental arrangements and procedures. As we shall see in chapter 3, this latter development has caused some investigators of memory to better understand something that some of us have accepted for a long time— that the differences between what learning theorists and memory theorists study can, to a significant extent, be defined by level of functioning, not only across ontogeny and phylogeny, but even within the intact adult person. The view I have just expressed will be one of the two or three main themes—perhaps the main one— throughout this book.

It will become obvious to you, and I will state from the outset, that I speak here as a partisan neobehaviorist. I will not, however, in these lectures, expound upon the history, and the virtues and vices, of the Hullian system, with which I am most identified; I will be trying to represent neobehaviorism more generally. Michael

Rashotte and I have written on Hull's sytematic position in a lengthy chapter in a handbook of psychology in the twentieth century (Amsel & Rashotte, 1977), and more recently in an extensive commentary in a book on Hull's theoretical papers (Amsel & Rashotte, 1984). The position I will try to represent has been misrepresented—insofar as it has not been neglected—in recent attacks on behaviorism and S-R interpretations of animal learning by those I will call the "cognitivists" and particularly the "animal cognitivists." I will emphasize and reemphasize the point that the attacks on, and defenses of, behaviorism almost always relate to the Skinnerian brand of radical behaviorism, and, as we shall see, that distinctions between this brand of behaviorism and neobehaviorism are almost never—if ever—made by the cognitivists. This I propose to address as an important second theme of this book.[1]

EXPERIMENTAL PSYCHOLOGY

A context in which my subject must be placed, albeit briefly, is experimental psychology. We are almost a decade past the centennial celebration of the founding of Wundt's laboratory in 1879, which is taken to be the centenary of the birth of experimental psychology. If we ask, what were the differences between experimental psychology in 1879 and 1979, we can properly answer in two ways: that these differences were immense, or that they were surprisingly small. It depends, of course, on the definition of ex-

---

[1]Kendler (1985) writes as follows in regard to the distinction between behaviorism and neobehaviorism, which I take to include Tolman's cognitive behaviorism. This distinction lies at the heart of my thesis.

An understanding of behaviorism demands an appreciation of the contributions of Edward Tolman's cognitive behaviorism and the neobehaviorism of Clark Hull, Kenneth Spence, and Neal Miller. It is an historical mistake to equate contemporary behaviorism with the methodological position and empirical program of Skinner and his followers. This admonition is not offered to minimize, in any way, the *enormous* contributions of radical behaviorism. Instead, it underlines the important point that Skinner's atheoretical position and views about social engineering are not core assumptions within behaviorism. (p. 123)

perimental psychology, but also on one's perspective. Is the question "What has become of experimental psychology?" or "What is left of it?"

One might almost say that, because of its growth and proliferation, there is no longer an identifiable, coherent experimental psychology. Building on the psychophysical and physiological contributions of Weber, Fechner, Müller, and Helmholtz, Wundt's experimental psychology (or physiological psychology, as he called it) was concerned, in what he thought to be a scientific and not a philosophical way, with the mind-body problem. Its subject matter was consciousness; it was based on the method of introspection; its elements were sensations; and it was the psychology of the "idealized"—not to say "idolized"—adult human. By 1929, the year the Society of Experimental Psychologists (SEP) founded by Titchener (a student of Wundt) was chartered in America, the definition had broadened. The composition of charter members included not only structuralists, who were the largest group and were students of Titchener, but also functionalists (e.g., Carr, Robinson) and even behaviorists (e.g., Lashley, Hunter). Experimental psychology in America had expanded to include not just psychophysics and sensory psychology, but also the functionalist subjects: learning and memory, motivation, emotion, the study of animals, and some acknowledgment of the importance of genetic, developmental, and comparative studies (the influences of Pavlov, Freud, and Darwin were now felt in experimental psychology). By 1979 experimental psychology was much less a distinct, identifiable discipline, and despite its growth, represented only a small part of psychology. In the American Psychological Association, which had been founded by experimentalists, the role of experimentalists had become almost "ceremonial," and the future of their substantial participation in the Association was uncertain. I doubt if one out of five young experimental psychologists was joining APA in 1979, or had even heard of SEP. In part, this was due to the formation of the Psychonomic Society in 1960, a result of the disaffection with APA of several of the leaders in experimental psychology. This organization was founded, in large part, to serve as a focus and a forum for whatever was left of a coherent experimental psychology. But in recent years, despite some efforts by biologically oriented investigators, the focus has been narrowing, and the Psychonomic Society meetings have become a forum primarily for work, mainly in the adult human, on what is nowadays called "cognitive psychology."

A parallel and perhaps not unrelated development has been that most experimentalists have come to favor even more specialized meetings: Examples are Vision Research, the Acoustical Society, the Societies for Neuroscience, Behavioral Genetics, and Developmental Psychobiology, the Cognitive Science Society, and the various "Winter Conferences," to name a few. These organizations define special-interest groups, and among the psychologists in them are those whose subjects bear some resemblance to what was originally experimental psychology, and those whose subjects do not; for example, between those whose approach is structuralist and those for whom functionalism is the approach. But despite these splits, these societies often provide the principal affiliation for those who would call themselves "experimental psychologists," even though these psychologists are part of a blend, and often a very small part, in these societies.

What this has meant is that the growth and broadening of experimental psychology has caused its fractionation, and its incorporation into a variety of scientific subdisciplines, some of which are of relatively recent origin. Many of the heroes of people who still call themselves experimental psychologists are, by training, non-psychologists: Examples are Chomsky, Sperry, Hubel, Wiesel, Kandel, and Simon. Indeed Simon (1980), a Nobel Laureate in economics, was selected to be the spokesman for behavioral scientists, including psychologists, on the 100th anniversary of the founding of the journal, *Science.*

The subjects investigated in structuralist laboratories in the early part of this century—psychophysics, sensory-physiological psychology, mental chronometry (reaction-time), imagery—are still with us, obviously with far more advanced investigative methods and techniques. These topics are now sometimes included under, but as we shall see are a very small part of, what is now called "cognitive psychology." In narrow respects, what is left of a strictly identifiable experimental psychology is what it began with; however, as we shall see, the composition of what is now called cognitive psychology or "human experimental psychology" is much broader, and very different, than it was.

Experimental psychology, in my opinion, is no longer a coherent discipline; it is nowadays split between the neurosciences and the cognitive (information) sciences, with some overlap between these two categories. (In the case of the neurosciences we now have topical areas that are forced to have names such as Developmental Neuropsychobiology and Developmental Neuropsychoethology.) This split is not, however, simply between those who study animals and those who study humans: Realignments (which I will detail later) are beginning to be apparent not only in what is now called human cognitive psychology but also in animal learning theory. Within the first grouping of interests, investigators of some traditional subjects such as memory, attention, and portions of the study of sensory processes and psycholinguistics, have allied their behavioral methods and concepts with neurological techniques in neuropsychological investigations. On the other hand, investigators of psychophysics, thinking and reasoning, concept formation, and the other parts of sensory psychology and psycholinguists appear to be making their principal contributions in conjunction with the information sciences, such as computer science and, more generally, human engineering. In the case of animal learning, the split is between associationistic and cognitive interpretations of behavior, but in a very different way from in the days of the Hull–Tolman debates. This recent version of such a split will be discussed in chapter 2.

THE COGNITIVE PSYCHOLOGISTS AND THE "ANIMAL COGNITIVISTS"

These preliminary remarks on the current status of experimental psychology have been offered as a first, coarse screening, leading to a better focus on the topic for these essays. I do not intend to pursue a further discussion of the history of experimental psychology, or even a history of learning theory. What I have been working toward is a critical review and commentary on the current and previous distinctions between behaviorism and cognitive psychology, with particular reference to the current split in learning theory among the views of the behaviorists, the neobehaviorists, and the animal cognitivists. I should like to present an account of my, perhaps idiosyncratic, understanding of the quite sudden (in scientific terms) disaffection with the behaviorist and neobehaviorist approaches that was at the root of the cognitive revolution, particularly as it involved these animal cognitivists, a group of learning theorists, who like the behaviorists and neobehaviorists, take the particulars for their theorizing almost exclusively from the behavior of the rat and the pigeon.

In general terms, my message will be along the following lines: It is a fact of history that, to take root and flourish, a newer point of view in any field of knowledge must be critical of an older, more established one. One can even accept that the criticisms of the older, by the newer approach, should involve a degree of mischaracterization and even misinformation, and of rediscovery of already-existing concepts. Whereas there are those who now believe that non-cumulative science is the modern way, most still favor the older view that knowledge in scientific areas should have a cumulative quality, as it does in most other intellectual disciplines. This quality, for example, is not a strong feature of some of the recent cognitive approaches to learning theory. This is largely because what are handed down by the animal cognitivists, often in the form of catch-phrases and stereotypes, are descriptions of earlier work and earlier ideas taken from secondary sources, sometimes misattributed and at times even incorrect.

In the broader field of "human cognitive psychology," as we shall see, the issues cannot be so finely drawn. The topics covered nowadays in this field are diverse and, with few exceptions (e.g., memory, psychophysics), are not ones that could have interested animal-learning theorists. But this is not a new point of view about the cognitivists, in contradistinction to the animal cognitivists. I expressed it almost three decades ago in a paper for an AAAS symposium that was published some years later (Amsel, 1965). This was in the context of a comparison of Tolman's cognitive neobehaviorism with the then "new" human cognitive psychology:

> [T]he cognitive theorists, generally speaking, have left the lower-level learning phenomena to the stimulus-response psychologists and have moved on to tackle more complex human behavior, usually involving language—a level of behavior for which their kind of theorizing was always more appropriate.
>
> Thus, what may appear as a rapprochement between S-R and cognitive points of view really doesn't amount to a rapprochement at all. It is simply that cognitive psychologists have, for the most part, moved into an area more appropriate to the meaning of the word *cognitive*: the study of the acquisition of knowledge by humans. Adherents to the older cognitive psychology of Tolman, applied to lower-level learning phenomena, seem to be scarce. The new cognitive psychology is a different animal: It is an attempt to describe cognitive processes in the language of the computer and information theory. It speaks not of demands, appetites, expectancies and readinesses but rather of inputs, outputs and channel capacities. "Plans" have replaced cognitive maps, but the plan seems a more exclusively human phenomenon. In place of means-ends-readinesses, and sign-Gestalt-expectations, there are bits and chunks of information to be "processed" by the organism. The new cognitivists and structuralists are questioning the vitality of stimulus-response psychology in much the same way the Gestaltists and older cognitivists did twenty years ago. (pp. 201-202)

In a less conciliatory statement about cognitive psychology in general, Denny (1986) recently has argued, in the words of his title, for the " 'Retention' of S-R in the Midst of the Cognitive Invasion." He points out that when S and R are appropriately defined so as to admit every sort of afferent and efferent event in their definition, we will have a consistent, objective basis for the explanation of behavior, avoid regression to a dualistic and mentalistic view of behavior, avoid the metaphorical and imprecise communication of the man-on-the-street, and reverse the fragmentation and lack of integration that results from the presence of two explanatory systems, one of which intrinsically lacks coherence. From this perspective, writes Denny, "an important difference between the traditional S-R view and the cognitive position is simply the kinds of problems currently being researched" (p. 47). His position is that when S and R are defined appropriately, these new kinds of problems will be seen not to require a new set of concepts—a new explanatory language. Denny's view is different from mine of some two decades earlier in that he sees the S-R explanatory language as powerful and appropriate for all research areas and, presumably, for all levels of processing. My view was, and has been, that the cognitive theorists "had moved on to tackle more complex human behavior . . . a level of behavior for which their kind of theorizing was always more appropriate" (1965, p. 202). But Denny's arguments, concerning the "metaphorical and imprecise language" of the cognitivists in general, hark back to Hull's views in his famous early papers in learning theory, and in renewing my acquaintance with those papers (Amsel & Rashotte, 1984), I found myself not entirely out of sympathy with what was to be Denny's recent, more uncompromising position. All this aside, the most important feature of Denny's statements is that they quite correctly juxtapose cognitive and S-R, not cognitive and behaviorism. As I will point out later, in more detail, cognitive and S-R are theoretical languages and strategies—both have been "behaviorisms" at one time or another.

Quite orthogonal to the issue of an appropriate theoretical language and notation is my earlier assertion that there appear to be no particular defining characteristics of the research areas to which the term cognitive psychology is now applied. (But this could always have been said about S-R psychology as well.) At least this is the case if one does not accept the definition attributed, perhaps apocryphally, to the founding editor of the journal, *Cognitive Psychology*, that cognitive psychology is "What I like." In some respects, of course, modern human cognitive psychology is a return to structuralism and even to introspection; in some respects it is a return to topics that interested psychologists before the days of the Grand Learning Theories; in some respects it is identified with psycholinguistics, a field whose birth coincided with and greatly strengthened the cognitive revolution in psychology; and in an important respect it has to do with the catch-all term "information processing," which came into prominence when Shannon and

Weaver's (1949) work on "information theory," a mathematical theory of communication, was, as Estes (1975b) points out, made accessible to psychologists. This latter influence was, of course, amplified by the advent of computers and the work on "artificial intelligence." The closest one can come to a more objective definition of "human cognitive psychology" is to review the tables of contents of relevant journals, and I have done this for the journals, *Cognition, Cognitive Psychology*, and *Cognitive Science*, each for a recent 10-year period. A compilation of the 21 research areas reflected in these contents, according to my non-expert reading of the titles, is presented in Table 1.

The top four entries—psycholinguistics, memory, problem-solving and cognitive development—make up over 50% of the 558 titles that entered the classification. The last 10 entries, comprising 12% of the total, are, in decreasing frequency: imagery (2.3); representation/cognitive maps (2.2); poetry/music (2.0); attention/reaction time (1.5); neurology of cognition (1.4); motivation/affect (0.7); associative learning (0.5); cognition in animals (0.5);

TABLE 1
Author's Classification of Articles in Cognitive Journals
Over a 10-Year Period[1]

Topics[2]	Cognitive Science	Cognitive Psychology	Cognition	Totals	Percent of Total
Psycholinguistics	28	33	95	156	28.0
Memory	8	38	16	62	11.1
Problem solving	10	27	10	47	8.4
Cognitive development	4	8	29	41	7.4
Theory Metatheory	25	0	8	33	5.9
Thinking Plans Reasoning	17	4	8	29	5.2
Concept formation	5	12	10	27	4.8
AI, Simulation Computer models	18	0	8	26	4.7
Perception	1	15	10	26	4.6

(Continued)

TABLE 1
(Continued)

Topics[2]	Cognitive Science	Cognitive Psychology	Cognition	Totals	Percent of Total
Reading					
Eye movements					
Feature ident.					
Visual search	8	9	9	6	4.6
Inference					
Prediction	2	14	3	19	3.4
Imagery	4	3	6	13	2.3
Representation					
Cognitive maps	5	4	3	12	2.2
Poetry					
Music	0	5	6	11	2.0
Attention, RT	0	6	2	8	1.5
Neurology & cog-					
nition	1	0	7	8	1.4
Motivation					
Affect	3	0	1	4	0.7
Cognition & lan-					
guage (animals)	0	0	3	3	0.5
Associative					
learning	0	0	3	3	0.5
Intelligence	0	0	2	2	0.4
Sensory					
Psychophysics	0	2	0	2	0.4
Totals	139	180	239	558	100

[1]The numbers in this table do not include book reviews, comments on articles, or rejoinders to these comments. In some cases in which the title made classification difficult, assignment was somewhat arbitrary. The classes themselves are also somewhat arbitrary and contain areas of overlap. It would obviously be possible to reduce (or increase) the number of classes, and consequently change their rank-order.

[2]In some cases, these headings include other areas as follows:

Memory: Melody, prose, and picture recognition; rehearsal; forgetting; recognition of faces; retrieval; spatial memory; encoding.

Psycholinguistics: Language; speech; sentence production; AMESLAN; analogy; narrative; metaphor.

Concept formation: Concept identification; classification; rules.

Problem solving: Decision processes; choice.

Inference: Intuition; diagnosis.

intelligence (0.4); sensory/psychophysics (0.4). (I also looked at *JEP: Learning, Memory and Cognition*, and, for the 10-year period, its contents reflected overwhelmingly articles on memory, with psycholinguistics running a fairly strong second.) The overlap between the subjects studied by human cognitive psychologists and by neobehaviorists is vanishingly small: Listed are three articles in associative learning and four in motivation and affect, together a little over 1% of the total. This simply strengthens the point I made earlier—that the cognitive revolution that began in the 1950s and early 1960s was a return to subjects for which the term "cognitive" was more appropriate, that it was not so much a revolution in theorizing as it was a revolution in subject matter—the particulars to which the theorizing was directed. This kind of statement can also be made, though perhaps with a little less force, about the overlap of subjects of the cognitive revolution of recent years and the subjects of the original experimental psychology.

BEHAVIORISM FROM THE STANDPOINT OF A NEOBEHAVIORIST

[A] fundamental assumption of cognitive psychology [is] that the unit of behavior is the "purposive action" rather than the "colorless movement" or "glandular squirt" of yesterday's behaviorists. (Bower, 1975, p. 27)

When the excited converts to a new intellectual movement are in full flight, even the best of them is given to occasional "jawboning" of this kind. Writing on "Cognitive Psychology: An Introduction" in the first of five volumes in *Handbook of Learning and Cognitive Processes* (Estes, 1975a), Bower offers this characterization of behaviorism. One must ask, "Which behaviorist does Bower's assertion describe?" Certainly not Tolman, whose most important book was titled *Purposive Behavior in Animals and Men*, and whose concepts of "cognitive map" and "sign-behavior-significate relationship" are as well defined and at least at the same level of analysis as the concept of "plan" that Bower favors. Does the statement describe the Hullian neobehaviorists: Hull, himself?

N. E. Miller? Mowrer? Spence? As an antidote to the effects of statements such as Bower's, I recommend to the impressionable reader articles from Hull (see Amsel & Rashotte, 1984) with titles such as "Knowledge and Purpose as Habit Mechanisms" (1930), and "Mind, Mechanism, and Adaptive Behavior" (1937); and a book by Dollard and Miller entitled, *Personality and Psychotherapy* (1950). My own neobehavioristic approach to understanding the mechanisms of frustration, suppression, persistence, and regression has nothing to do with "colorless movements" or "glandular squirts." Any behaviorist who is concerned with needs, drives, appetites, demands, expectancies, anticipations; with rewards and frustrations, punishments and reliefs, is *ipso facto* concerned with "purposive action." (Indeed it may fairly be said that purposive action is not a particular feature of today's cognitive psychology.) Nevertheless a statement like this, made by a highly respected scientist, who is also the co-author, with Hilgard, of perhaps the most influential textbook in learning theory, must have had great force in the thinking of those younger partisans of the cognitive revolution. Many of these young scientists had never been exposed to the relevant history, and having been influenced by such a statement from such an authority, were not likely ever to expose themselves to it.

As we shall see, Bower's seemingly offhand description of behaviorism does not come close to fitting even J. B. Watson's original (1913/1919) position, let alone the neobehaviorism that followed. I would like now to "flash back" to Watson's position.

From Watson to Behaviorism at 75

With the shift in emphasis from behavior to the acquisition of information as the object of psychological study, investigators, not only of human cognition (our recent example) but also of animal cognition, took it as a requirement of their new faith to rationalize their conversion. The object of their disavowal was, of course, Behaviorism, in the person of its archetype, J. B. Watson, and his major contemporary representative, B. F. Skinner. My purpose now is to extract the essence of the behaviorist position in the form of Watson's views in *Psychology from the Standpoint of a Behaviorist* (1919).

Skinner (1959) judged this book to be Watson's most important, and my inference is that he takes it to reflect, or be the forerunner of, his own position. Better than any other of Watson's writings, I think, *Psychology* reflects the original modest tenets of the "behaviorist revolution." A more specific thesis of mine in these lectures is that the definition of psychology these tenets require is still a very acceptable one. I will argue that what came in the 1930s and later to be called "neobehaviorism" was very much like what Watson was advocating in his earlier (1913/1919) statements, and that the later, more doctrinaire Watson of the book, *Behaviorism* (1925/1930), does not represent any behaviorism since that time. A possible exception is Skinner's, starting about 1950, but not Skinner's behaviorism in *Behavior of Organisms* (1938). It is also my strong position that contemporary references to behaviorism by cognitivists do not as a rule address the distinction between behaviorism and neobehaviorism, and are misleading about the tenets of neobehaviorism and of early Watsonian behaviorism, and the intellectual climate out of which they arose. A very good example is Schwartz and Lacey's book, *Behaviorism, Science, and Human Nature* (1982), in which Skinner is identified, quite correctly, as "the leading figure in behavior theory" and as "the spokesman for the discipline" (p. 226). And a particularly telling statement in this regard occurs early in the book: "What distinguishes behavior theory is . . . that an analysis of how environmental events affect behavior will tell us all we need to know about the determinants of action" (pp. 14-15). This may indeed characterize the behaviorism of post-1950 Skinner and the later Watson, but it does not characterize Tolmanian, Hullian, or other brands of neobehaviorism; it particularly does not characterize the fundamental behaviorism of the Watson of 1913/1919.

Watson's *Psychology* (1919) starts with a metatheoretical introduction and the message is, of course, the new Behaviorism, which had been enunciated in 1913 in a paper, considered to be the Behaviorist Manifesto, "Psychology as the Behaviorist Views It." Consequently, in the spirit of that classic paper, the book, unlike, for example, Titchener's *A Text-Book of Psychology* (1910), carefully omits terms and language connoting mentalism. In other respects, however, the chapters that follow, on methods, the various sense organs, the motor systems, emotions, instincts, habit, thinking, and memory, cover the same topics as other psychology textbooks of the time.

Behavioristic psychology, as Watson saw it, recognized that "the differences among the various sciences . . . [were] only those necessitated by a division of labor" (p. vii). In this sentiment, expressed in prefatory remarks, he anticipated the main premise in Pratt's *The Logic of Modern Psychology* (1939), written 20 years later. Pratt's title was an obvious play on Bridgman's *The Logic of Modern Physics* (1927), which promoted the "operational character of concepts" as a way of dealing with the more relative nature of knowledge in the move from Newtonian to Einsteinian physics. Operational definition became the catchword, and to some extent the hallmark, of experimental psychology in the 1940s and 1950s. The differences among sciences, according to Watson (and later, Pratt), are only those dictated by the different constructions of the world emerging out of the objectively verifiable perceptions of observers with different interests. His strong position was that it should take no special training (of the Titchenerian variety) to be an observer, that the special training removed from the observer an essential naiveté, and that this special kind of observation, introspection, was in principle unverifiable and therefore unscientific.

Reading the first chapter of Watson's *Psychology* ("Problems and Scope of Psychology"), and the 1913 paper, brings one face to face with the differences between the positions taken by the 1913/1919 Watson and the other early behaviorists, and the later caricatures of Watsonian behaviorism. The arch-environmentalist, Watson, refers to hereditary (explicit and implicit) responses; the muscle-twitch, switchboard psychologist says "we can leave out . . . [comparisons of] the action of the central nervous system with . . . electric switchboards, and the like"; the founding behaviorist who gave us the "colorless movement" and the "glandular squirt" says that to prepare for psychology, learn your physiology, experimental zoology and pharmacology, spend some time (as an observer) in the psychiatric clinic, learn something about business and law, and get some training in statistical methods. In some of these last respects, the ones having to do with practicality and application, Watson and The Behaviorist of our generation, B. F. Skinner, are much alike; in other respects—physiology and statistics—they are of course very different. But remember this was the earlier Watson, the Watson who summarized and represented the essential behaviorism of his time, and who anticipated the broader neobehaviorist movement that was to follow. In a later book (*Behaviorism*, 1925, revised 1930), after polarization had occurred and systematic lines had been drawn, and Watson was no longer a member of the academic community, we were to see a more doctrinaire Watson. In describing the controversy that Watson's post-1919 writings aroused, Skinner (1959) writes that "Watson's taste for, and skill in, polemics led him into extreme positions from which he never escaped" (p. 191). It is only to this side of Watson's writings that the catch phrases of yesterday and today can properly be directed. I should like to take a moment to emphasize this point in relation to other parts of Watson's (1919) *Psychology*.

Methods, for Watson, fell into four categories: observation (direct and with the use of instruments), conditioned reflex (secretion and motor), *verbal reports of all kinds*, and psychological tests. The emphasis was on objectivity, and the instructor, in a footnote, was advised to demonstrate in the classroom a series of not-very-revolutionary, functionalist methods: the recording of respiration and motor changes, a word-association test, recording of eye movements in reading, the army alpha test. The new "revolutionary" behaviorism had no elementism or "muscle-twitchism"—no "colorless movement" or "glandular squirt"—about it, and involved no new methods—a historical fact that repeats itself in the relative absence of new methods in the more recent cognitive revolution in psychology.

Watson dealt with emotions and instincts as "hereditary modes of response." The well-known Watsonian trio of emotional responses, fear, rage, and love (not mentalistic terms for Watson because, I suppose, he thought them closely tied to behavior), were described as part of "the original and fundamental nature of man." (These are hardly the writings of an arch-environmentalist.) What is most remarkable is Watson's adherence to the view that these emotional responses are instinctive, hereditary patterns of behavior and his preference for a "genetic" (in the older sense of developmental) approach to their investigation. This functionalist emphasis on "genetic psychology" is a strong feature of Watson's behaviorism and characterizes his famous experiment with Rayner (1920) which, without stretching things much, can be regarded as the cradle of conditioning and behavior therapies. For learning theorists, the concept and the substance of the "conditioned emotional response" of Estes and Skinner (1941), and the conditioned suppression paradigm so favored by the animal cognitivists, can also be found in Watson and Rayner's work with Albert and his conditioned fear of—or suppression of approach to—white furry objects (Watson and Rayner used the term "conditioned emotional reaction"). Nor is there a great theoretical distance between these characterizations of emotions in early Watson and the conceptualizations of conditioned emotional and incentive-motivational states by the (Hullian) neobehaviorists (e.g., N. E. Miller, O. H. Mowrer, J. S. Brown) and by the other major stream of modern Pavlovians represented by R. L. Solomon and his students.

Watson on Heredity and Environment: The Concepts of Instinct and Habit

Watson (1919) acknowledged the importance of both heredity and learning, as the theories of both Tolman and Hull did later. "In instinct," Watson writes, "the pattern and order are inherited, in habit both are acquired during the lifetime of the individual" (p. 273). Noteworthy also in the context of Watson's treatment of instinct and habit are the following: (a) Watson's obvious commitment to the developmental ("genetic") approach: He describes the development of eye-hand coordination in a child from the 80th to the 171st day of life, and reaching for a candle from the 150th to the 220th day, (b) Watson's alliance of behaviorism with physiology: He discusses the importance of kinesthesis in sequential habits, the possibility that late in training cortical function may be replaced by activity at lower centers, a kind of short-circuiting process not at all out of line with current neurophysiological thinking, and he has reference to the work of Franz and Lashley on what came to be known as equipotentiality of cortical function. This emphasis on neurophysiology, along with his very extensive treatment of receptors and effectors in earlier chapters, makes it obvious that, when as astute a historian and philosopher of science as Bergmann (1956), in his essay "The Contribution of J. B. Watson," wrote: "Watson had an amazingly naive and almost superstitious distrust of any appeal to the action of the central nervous system" (p. 273), he had to be referring to Watson's later more polemical positions. Such a characterization clearly does not fit the 1913/1919 Watson—the Watson who was the driving force behind the behaviorist movement, and who, as I have claimed, is emulated in the neobehaviorists. Let us look further: (c) Under the heading "determiners of acts" Watson described what Hull later called the "habit-family hierarchy." He concluded that, of a large number of possible responses to a stimulus, the one that will occur depends on, in order (1) recency, (2) frequency, (3) context, what he termed the "general setting of the situation as a whole," (4) a factor which I will call "recently induced set," (5) temporary "intra-organic" (motivational) factors, and (6) the life history of the individual. (Much of this sounds remarkably like Tolman.) But what stands out most clearly in Watson's discussion of habits is that there was nothing of the "building-blocks" about it: The concept in 1919 was more Thorndikian than Pavlovian. As Skinner (1959) pointed out, Watson's rejection of mentalism was greatly influenced by Lloyd Morgan (and, as Pratt [1939, pp. 9-10] has written, by James and Jennings), and his concept of habit by Thorndike's trial-and-error learning (as, obviously, was Skinner's concept of the operant).

What we see in the 1919 textbook, then, are what we glimpsed in the 1913 "Manifesto." There is, first, a strong emphasis on application: As B. F. Skinner, the modern arch-behaviorist, has been for our generation, Watson was, in many ways, the applied psychologist of his generation (and this even before he went to work for the J. Walter Thompson advertising agency). This becomes more explicit in the preface to the second edition of his *Psychology* (1924), in which "modern psychology" is called upon to "solve the problems that come from living in complex groups" (p. xi). This psychology can do, Watson says, by throwing off philosophy and the academic tradition and finding a way to "seek its facts in the daily lives of human beings." Second, the picture we have of Watson as a radical environmentalist, mainly on the basis of his "Give me a dozen healthy infants . . ." statement and his discarding of instinct and down-playing of heredity in his book, *Behaviorism* (1925/1930), is not at all a characteristic of the 1919 book (revised 1924), as it was not of his 1913 paper or of his Columbia lectures that were published as *Behavior: An Introduction to Comparative Psychology* (1914). As a matter of fact, Watson's classic "brag" in the 1925 book ends with this not-often-quoted sentence: "I am going beyond my facts and I admit it, but so have the advocates of the contrary, and they have been doing it for thousands of years" (p. 273). Skinner's (1966) comment on this was, "As an enthusiastic specialist in the psychology of learning [Watson] went beyond his facts to emphasize what could be done in spite of genetic limitations" (p. 1205). (Was Skinner telling us something about his own environmentalism?) Third, as we have seen, Watson's original concept of habit was Thorndikian and gave way to a more Pavlovian emphasis in the 1925/1930 book, *Behaviorism*, although the seeds of a conditioned-reflex approach would seem to have been sown in his presidential address to APA, "The Place of the Conditioned Reflex in Psychology," published in 1916. It was only later, when he appeared to become a thoroughgoing Pavlovian, that the "building-blocks" characterization of complex habits, not a feature of the earlier Watson, emerged. Such a characterization, incidentally, would be apt for recent work at the cellular level in Aplysia reviewed by Hawkins and Kandel (1984), whose metaphor for building blocks was a "cell-biological alphabet." "Building blocks" would also be an apt characterization for recent connectionist computer models of cognitive function (e.g., Feldman & Ballard, 1982).

Many contemporary neobehaviorists, like Tolman and Hull before them, as we shall see, do not subscribe to the more radical behaviorism of the Watson of 1925/1930; but whether they realize it or not, they do subscribe to the Watson of 1913 and 1919, whose message was quite simple—a reasonable and pragmatic level of objectivity and verifiability in psychology, as in all science. And this—and not "colorless movements" and "glandular squirts"—is finally, manifestly, Watson's legacy to contemporary neobehaviorism: his insistence that behavior, and not the introspectively revealed mental event, is the datum of psychology. As Kimble writes in his *Conditioning and Learning* (1961), "[Watson's early position] was an objective, association psychology, with an emphasis upon habit, biological in viewpoint and analytic in approach" (p. 23). The love affair of psychologists with formal operational definition and the unity of science came years after Watson's own infatuation with these conceptions, which had, already in Watson's time, been around more informally for many years.

BEHAVIORISTS AND BEHAVIORISMS

There have been several reasonably distinct versions of behaviorism. The seminal one is, of course, Watson's early (1913/1919) version, which was modified and hardened in 1925, to its detriment, most agree. There followed Tolman's purposive or molar behaviorism of the 1920s and 1930s; the operational behaviorism of the 1930s and 1940s—Pratt, Stevens, early Skinner, Hull, Bergmann, Spence, and others—which appears to have been anticipated by Watson in 1919 and in Lashley's later articles; and the most recent, the radical (descriptive) behaviorism of later Skinner, which can be dated from the famous article, "Are Theories of Learning Necessary?" (1950). This last version, which Skinner shows some signs of softening in some of his more recent writings, most resembles the later, more doctrinaire Watsonian behaviorism. (And, like Watson's, Skinner's earlier position, exemplified by his *Behavior of Organisms* [1938], was not as radical a behaviorism as his later one.) In many respects, the behaviorism of Hull, with its emphasis on stimulus-response, habit, unlearned S-R connections, adaptiveness of behavior, physiology, its admonitions to guard against subjectivism and anthropomorphism, and its preference for S-R analyses of terms such as anxiety, purpose, and anticipation—is most like the 1913/1919 Watson (see Amsel & Rashotte, 1984). A historical note in this regard: Watson (1913) acknowledged that his definition of behaviorism was anticipated by W. B. Pillsbury, who was Hull's teacher at Michigan.

But then the behaviorism of Hull's arch theoretical rival, Tolman, was (except that he thought Watson's behaviorism too molecular) also very close to the 1913/1919 Watson; and, except for the flavor of the intermediate constructs, and from the perspective of some 40 years, it was virtually the same as Hull's. Here are introductory passages from Tolman's most important work, *Purposive Behavior in Animals and Men* (1932). I present this material from Tolman in juxtaposition to the view of many contemporary cognitive theorists of animal learning that *behavior is simply the vehicle for understanding the minds of animals*. Tolman wrote:

> The motives which lead to the assertion of a behaviorism are simple. All that can ever actually be observed in fellow human beings and in lower animals is behavior. Another organisms's private mind, if he have any, can never be got at. And even the supposed ease and obviousness of "looking within" and observing one's own mental processes, directly and at first hand, have proved, when subjected to laboratory control, in large part chimerical; the dictates of "introspection" have been shown over and over again to be artifacts of the particular laboratory in which they were obtained.
>
> The behaviorism here to be presented will contend that mental processes are most usefully to be conceived as but dynamic aspects, or determinants, of behavior. They are functional variables which intermediate in the causal equation between environmental stimuli and initiating physiological states or excitements, on the one side, and final overt behavior, on the other.
>
> Further, it is to be pointed out that although behaviorism exerts an emotional appeal because it appears radical, modern and simple, actually we shall find it recondite, difficult, but, we may hope, scientific. (p. 2)

And, from a later passage, Tolman again:

> For the behaviorist, "mental processes" are to be identified and defined in terms of the behaviors to which they lead. "Mental processes" are, for the behaviorist, naught but inferred determinants of behavior, which ultimately are deducible from behavior. Behavior and these inferred determinants are both objectively defined types of entity. There is about them, the behaviorist would declare, nothing private or "inside." Organisms, human and sub-human, are biological entities immersed in environments. To these environments

they must, by virtue of their physiological needs, adjust. Their "mental processes" are functionally defined aspects determining their adjustments. For the behaviorist all things are open and above-board; for him, animal psychology plays into the hands of human psychology. (p. 3)

ATTACKS ON BEHAVIORISM

Give me a dozen healthy infants, well-formed, and my own special world to bring them up in and I'll guarantee to take any one at random and train him to become any type of specialist I might select—doctor, lawyer, artist, merchant chief and, yes, even beggarman and thief, regardless of his talents, penchants, tendencies, abilities, vocations, and race of his ancestors. I am going beyond my facts and I admit it, but so have the advocates of the contrary, and they have been doing it for thousands of years. (Watson, from *Behaviorism*, 1930, p. 104)

Contemporary reactions to behaviorism are often directed at the extreme environmentalism reflected in the first sentence of this passage from Watson's *Behaviorism* (the second sentence, as I have claimed, is seldom mentioned). The main attacks, however, are directed against Skinner's later brand of behaviorism. These reactions have come from a variety of well-known quarters. Those from outside of laboratory psychology, on close examination, are directed not so much against the message of early philosophical behaviorism, but rather against almost any version of a scientific approach in psychology. (Some of these attacks on behaviorism could as easily be directed at Wundt and Titchener.) Here are some examples: When Carl Rogers (1964) criticizes behaviorism in the book, *Behaviorism and Phenomenology*, it is the reaction of a phenomenologist and humanist against laboratory psychology and the idea that science can be impersonal. When the founding psycholinguists (Chomsky, G. Miller, and others) attack behaviorism the argument seems to be by nativists against scientific empiricism: They are reacting against *Skinner's* environmentalism and determinism, and, specifically, against any possibility that learning and reinforcement can be involved in the acquisition of language. And when the novelist, Arthur Koestler, in his *The Act of*

Creation (1964), attacks behaviorism, he seems to be expressing his distaste, not uncommon in humanists who are otherwise friendly toward science, for the very idea that a science of *complex* human behavior is even possible. ("How can anyone understand my marvelous brain?")

The attacks on behaviorism from within the pale of laboratory psychology are a little more difficult to characterize. There is seldom a quarrel with objectivism, although a keen ear can sense the stirrings in some quarters of a return to introspective methods. Nor is it a matter of choosing between pure and applied science: Many behaviorists, certainly Watson and Skinner, clearly have embodied both interests. If it has to do with what the psychologist does in the laboratory, it is not even always about some preferred area of investigation; as we have seen and shall see, many of the attacks on behaviorism and S-R psychology—they are seldom differentiated—come nowadays from investigators in the field of animal learning. If there is a disagreement between the positions of the behaviorists (including neobehaviorists) and these animal cognitivists, it is that the former invent constructs to explain behavior, whereas for the latter behavior in itself is said to be unimportant except as a "window on the mind." But many of today's animal cognitivists would not agree with this assertion of mine, mainly because they appear to have forgotten that most behaviorists and all neobehaviorists, like most scientists, theorize in terms of mediating constructs. In order for most of their arguments to have any validity, the defining characteristics of behaviorism must be restricted to the extreme, doctrinaire positions of the later Watson and of Skinner's "Are Theories of Learning Necessary?" If we accept that there are, and have been, other, less radical behaviorisms than Skinner's, the disagreement between these neobehaviorists and the animal-learning cognitivists is, as I have claimed, between explaining behavior and studying the mind; the older disagreement *among* neobehaviorists was about the explanatory power and rigor of the stimulus-response and the cognitive *theories*. The latter kind of disagreement was the one between Hull and Tolman; the former, in my view, is the fundamental disagreement that led to behaviorism itself. As we have seen, Watson himself was comfortable with operational definitions of states such as fear and anger. What made him (and what makes neobehaviorists) uncomfortable was treating as scientific data the product of the direct examination of such states by the only person who could experience them.

There can be little disagreement with the fact that—to use our earlier parliamentary metaphor—behaviorism, usually in the form of stimulus-response psychology, was once the government, but has long since become the minority party; and that cognitive psychology, once the loyal opposition, is now clearly the government. In spite of this fact, the leaders of this new cognitive government cannot seem to break the habit of acting like the opposition party. Here is a recent example: Writing as the representative of the social and behavioral sciences, in the centennial issue of the journal, *Science*, H. A. Simon (1980) characterizes behaviorism as "suited to the predominantly positivistic and operationalist views of the methodology and philosophy of science . . ." and as "[preoccupied with] laboratory rats rather than humans engaged in complex thinking and problem-solving tasks" (p. 76). Again, here, Simon has stated the case against behaviorism in terms of intellectual complexity, and the "rat versus human" version of the humanist argument. The 1919 Watson would not have been—and no philosophical behaviorist or neobehaviorist can be—happy with Simon's characterization of behaviorism, because the concern of behaviorists was and is, at bottom, really only with objectivity and verifiability. Even though a preference for the S-R theoretical notation over a cognitive one may predispose the theorist to more modest explanatory domains, it is not one's systematic preference—structuralism or functionalism, S-R behaviorism or cognitivism—that determines, *in principle*, the level of complexity that can be understood. Even Watson, in the 1913/1919 version of his position, was surely interested in how "heart and nerve and sinew," to borrow a phrase from Kipling, work in between stimulus and response. With his emphasis on the unity of science, objectivity, physiology, genetics (in our sense) and development, I think Watson (and certainly, Hull) would have been more attuned to neuroscience-oriented than to cognitive science-oriented psychology, but would not have seen this as a choice related to complexity of subject-matter. Watson's reaction to some of the original claims for artificial intelligence might have reciprocated Simon's to behaviorism. They might have seemed to him a kind of introspection mediated by computer.

No phyletic limitation and no level of complexity is ruled out for behavioristic analysis: Watson was certainly interested in complex processes in humans, and, as we shall see, such an interest has been a strong feature of the work of most "rat" and some "pigeon" psychologists. I think it a misreading of Watsonian, Tolmanian, Hullian, and even Skinnerian behaviorism to say, as Simon does, that behaviorism "[confined] experimental psychology to relatively simple memory and learning experiments . . ." (p. 76). It is true, for example, that neobehaviorists like Tolman and Hull were focused on motivational and incentive factors and on the specific parameters of conditioning and learning in a way that current human cognitive psychology is not (see Amsel, 1965); but although most of their work was not with concepts related to higher mental function, you can, for example, find in Tolman (1948) an extensive treatment of "cognitive maps"; in Hull (1935) such non-simple applications of S-R theory as solutions to Maier's "reasoning" problems, and Köhler's description of the chimpanzee Sultan's spontaneous use of tools; in N. E. Miller (1935) a stimulus-response analysis of "insight"; and in K. W. Spence (1937) a stimulus-response analysis of transposition. (I recommend the latter three papers to anyone who is looking for complexity in stimulus-response behavioristic analysis.)

To conclude, however, I come back again to my major concern in these lectures, which is not so much with the differences between neobehaviorism and cognitivism in general as with the differences between neobehaviorism and the new animal cognitivism.

It is something of a paradox—certainly it would be contrary to the perception of most dispassionate observers—that the rejection of behaviorism (and neobehaviorism) is sometimes more complete in the animal cognitivists than in cognitivists whose subjects are people. While it is true, as H. H. Kendler (1987, p. 380) writes, that "some cognitivists have rejected methodological behaviorism . . . from their conviction that cognitive psychology represents a complete revolutionary break with behaviorism," there are those, as

Kendler also points out, who do not regard behaviorism and cognitivism as completely incompatible "global paradigms." An example of the latter class of cognitivists is G. Mandler, who is not an animal cognitivist, but who can sound remarkably like Tolman:

> We [cognitive psychologists] have not returned to the methodologically confused position of the late nineteenth century, which cavalierly confused introspection with theoretical processes and theoretical processes with conscious experience. Rather, many of us have become methodological behaviorists in order to become good cognitive psychologists. (1979, p. 281)

This kind of statement does, I believe, characterize many cognitivists who study people in the laboratory. It does not, however, characterize the attitude of the majority of animal cognitivists. For example, Dickinson (1979), in reviewing an influential anthology, *Cognitive Processes in Animal Behavior* (Hulse, Fowler, & Honig, 1978), characterizes the contributors' rejection of behaviorism in the following words: "[A]ccording to the concensus view expressed in this book, behavior is but a spade to disinter thought . . ." (p. 553).[2]

---

[2]The larger quote from which this is taken refers to Guthrie's famous quip about Tolman's cognitive theory leaving the rat "buried in thought." Dickinson (1979) writes that "the jibe no longer stings, for the focus of interest has changed; according to the concensus view expressed in this book, behavior is but a spade to disinter thought, and the mistake made by the traditional cognitive theorists in their battle with S-R theory was to assume that the two enterprises had a common focus" (p. 553). In the book review from which the above quote was taken, Dickinson separates himself from behaviorism and assumes the role of spokesman for animal cognitivism in these words: "When the psychological community at large abandoned the behaviorist perspective, the traditional learning theories died a natural death" (p. 551). It has been drummed into us again and again that theories do not die natural deaths, but are in time replaced by better theories. It was not clear in 1979, and it is not now, what these better theories were, unless one is referring to the Rescorla-Wagner model of 1972, which was a better theory for some facets of Pavlovian conditioning, particularly for the idea of shared associative strength, but which was in no sense in its essence a cognitive theory; it was pure associationism.

Perhaps what we see when we compare the cognitivists and the animal cognitivists, with respect to their attitudes toward behaviorism, is what the psychoanalysts might regard as a familiar kind of dynamics: The closer the relationship the more complete the break from that relationship when it comes, and the more it is rationalized and justified.

In the next chapter, I will attempt a description and a comparison of the "old" and the "new" learning theory, both of which are based almost entirely on the study of laboratory animals. My purpose will be to examine them from a somewhat more inclusive perspective than is usually taken, and to give a very brief account of the factors that contributed to their existence; of what they were and are about; and of how they are the same and different.

2

Issues Surrounding the Old and the New Learning Theory

. . . why abandon a belief
Merely because it ceases to be true.
Cling to it long enough, and not a doubt
It will turn true again, for so it goes.
Most of the change we think we see in life
Is due to truths being in and out of favor.
—Robert Frost "The Black Cottage"[1]

THE "OLD" LEARNING THEORY: WHAT WAS IT ABOUT?

When, some 20 years ago, the "cognitive revolution" was already well underway, the lines that were drawn by the neo-cognitivists were indeed, as Simon (1980) wrote, and as I wrote earlier (Amsel, 1965), between investigations involving humans and animals as subjects. When the work involved people as the laboratory subject, psychologists were, of course, concerned with processes they regarded as primarily human: remembering and forgetting of verbal material—and later of visual and auditory material—processing

---

[1]I am indebted to Robert W. Jackman for calling my attention to these lines of poetry.

of information, perception, imaging, simulation of human problem solving by computers, formation and identification of concepts, reading, language; it is subjects such as these that still define human cognitive psychology (see Table 1). On the other hand, as we have seen, a number of eminent psychologists had for many years taken the experimental particulars from which they derived their theories from observation of, and experimentation with, nonhuman animals. Many if not most of these learning theorists were less interested in the cognitive and intellectual abilities of the animals they studied than in the underlying learning processes, such as Pavlovian conditioning and instrumental (Thorndikian) learning, and in basic motivational or need systems. In short, they were involved in the scientific investigation of the more primitive processes, ontogenetically as well as phylogenetically, and *in this sense* in the more simple kinds of learning that operate *not only in animals but in people as well*. Both Hull and Tolman, two of the leading learning theorists of the 1930s and 1940s, introduced into psychology theoretical systems that had as one of their concerns the identification of the factors which contributed to the formation of habits and goal expectancies, and with the complementary motivational concepts of need, drive, and demand. Hull, for example, was tremendously preoccupied with the mechanisms of adaptation and survival. Even in his most formal theorizing, in *Principles of Behavior* (1943), there are several references to these concepts, and they form a dominant theme in his earlier seminal papers (Amsel & Rashotte, 1984), and in his last book, *A Behavior System* (1952).

The next generation of learning theorists—H. F. Harlow, N. E. Miller, O. H. Mowrer, B. F. Skinner, and K. W. Spence—carried on a tradition of experimental research and theory in which the aim was to understand the basic associative and motivational processes of humans by studying and understanding these same processes in lower animals. Or so, at least, it has seemed to me. True, Skinner's work with pigeons has given us a tremendous increase in our understanding of the ways of the pigeon; but obviously Skinner has been interested in pigeons more abstractly, as an animal model for the experimental analysis of behavior. Harlow's later work was primarily with monkeys, and this work has contributed greatly to the knowledge we have about the effects of rearing practices upon emotional-affectional systems of monkeys. But, clearly, this was not Harlow's only, or even primary, intention; the purpose of Harlow's work was to understand developmental influences on affectional (and other) systems in people. As I suggested over a quarter century ago (Amsel, 1961), at about the time the cognitive revolution began, one of the characteristics of most of the American learning theorists who had worked with animals in the preceding quarter century (or more) was that they had not been interested in the animals they were studying in the way a naturalist is, but rather had been interested in these animals as "preparations" from which it might be possible to develop hypotheses about associative and motivational-emotional processes of mammals in general and humans in particular. It is for this reason that the early applications of the work on anxiety, conflict, and frustration to psychopathology and the behavioral therapies come not from research in human learning but from the work in animal learning (e.g. , Amsel, 1958, 1971; Brown & Farber, 1951; Dollard & Miller, 1950; Miller, 1944; Mowrer, 1939).

Up to about the late 1960s, it would have been fair to say that learning theorists who based their ideas on work with animals (usually the pigeon, rat, or monkey) were at least as interested in the conative and affective aspects of behavior as in the cognitive aspect, *and they were seldom interested in the pigeon, rat, or monkey.* They tended to be functionalist in outlook and to be influenced by Darwin, by Pavlov, and by Freud in their emphasis on adaptiveness, on motivation and reinforcement, and on the nonintentional nature of an important part of learning and personality. On the other hand, psychologists who were students of human learning and memory tended to be more fascinated by the associative-cognitive aspects of behavior, and showed very little interest in the conative or affective. There seemed then to be within their ranks more of an even split between functionalist and structuralist outlook: The ones who studied "human learning" (e.g., Postman, Underwood) were functionalists; those who studied "memory" (e.g., Mandler, Tulving) were structuralists and cognitivists, and among the great number and variety of their intellectual ancestors Darwin, Pavlov, and Freud would not have been dominant figures.

THE "NEW" LEARNING THEORY:
HOW IS IT DIFFERENT?

Things have changed. It now seems obvious to me, and to others I am sure, that learning theory, the kind that has been based almost exclusively on the rat and the pigeon, has gone in two directions. One direction is away from the older conative and affective concerns, and from S-R associationism and behaviorism, and toward what is called "information processing," or more popularly, "animal cognition." The second direction is toward neuroscience. It also seems obvious to me that at least in one neuroscience area, investigations of the neuropsychology of memory, the older approach, which I will call stimulus-response, and the newer cognitive approach seem to have found a way to live together. I will come back to this point later.

On the other hand, and somewhat paradoxically, recent cognition-based animal learning theory has been resistant to such a marriage. (In a recent letter, a colleague of this persuasion, trying to recruit a graduate student, wrote, "The goal of my research is to narrow the gap between animal and human cognition." I'm not sure if by making pigeons smarter or people dumber.) I would reemphasize the point that, unlike Tolman, these neocognitivists now regard behavior simply as a vehicle for understanding thinking in animals. Two of the interesting features of this approach are that behavior per se is said to be less important than it used to be; and that, again unlike Tolman but as in the human learning and memory work, emotion and motivation are virtually ignored. (Indeed in a recent book entitled *Animal Cognition* [Roitblat, Bever, & Terrace, 1984] reference to Tolman occurs in only 4 out of 34 chapters.) The fathers of our troubled science, following more-or-less standard philosophical practice, were comfortable with a definition of psychology that included the cognitive, the affective, and the conative. In recent years it has seemed that, for many if not most psychologists, the definition included only the cognitive.

How can a cognitive psychology—animal or human—account for the fact that when a person is agitated by anxiety, he or she will eat more (or less)? Or that when animals are shocked and are in a state of residual emotionality they will drink more water (Amsel & Maltzman, 1950; Siegel & Siegel, 1949) or eat more food (Siegel & Brantley, 1951)? Or that when a rat is running to escape cues that have been paired with shock and is also hungry, it will run faster than if not hungry (Amsel, 1950), even though hunger is irrelevant in the situation? The effects of what Hull called the drive properties of need states have no account in cognitive formulations, and I dare to assert that they and other such effects cannot simply be left out of accounts of behavior. And effects such as these, and many others, would not, either, appear to be promising behavioral phenomena from which to infer thinking or other mental operations.

The decline of the conative and affective (and the ascendancy of the cognitive) were antedated and abetted by five apparently unrelated theoretical influences. The first was Hebb's (1949) rejection of the drive concept in his book, *The Organization of Behavior*, in which the constantly active Hebbian cell did not require a motivating force to put it into action. (The report in the same year of the discovery of the brain-stem reticular formation [Morruzi & Magoun, 1949] later caused a change in Hebb's thinking, and he added a concept of drive [arousal] to what he called his "Conceptual Nervous System" [Hebb, 1955]). The second influence was Skinner's concept of the operant, which required reinforcers, but of emitted rather than evoked behaviors. His paper "Are Theories of Learning Necessary?" (Skinner, 1950) relegated Hullian concepts like drive and need to a category Skinnerians liked to call "spooky." The third factor in this decline, again right around mid-century, was the influence of the statistical or stochastic learning theories of Estes (1950) and Bush and Mosteller (1951), which provided no accommodation for parameters representing motivation or affect. (Incidentally, the more recent influential mathematical model of conditioning by Rescorla and Wagner [1972] has no place for these concepts either.) It obviously occurred to Estes that this was a shortcoming of the statistical approach, because he later (Estes, 1958) attempted to introduce drive into his stimulus-sampling theory in the form of a separate population of stimulus elements. Unfortunately, so far as I am aware, this attempt remained an elegant exercise in theorizing, and was not followed up. The fourth and fifth factors came a decade later in the form of the new field of psycholinguistics and the work of Hubel and Wiesel on receptive fields in vision. Many would date the conception of psycholinguistics to Chomsky's (1959) review of Skinner's (1957) book, *Verbal Behavior*; the birth to G. A. Miller's (1962) paper on the psychological study of grammar; and the confirmation to Neisser's book (1967) *Cognitive Psychology*. Psycholinguistics, which became a powerful force in the new cognitive psychology, was no more generous in providing living space for concepts representing drive or affect. Finally, Hubel and Wiesel's (1962) seminal paper, which characterized the elements of the visual receptive field as bars and edges, was taken as support for a rampaging cognitive structuralism which put further into eclipse the functionalist concepts of motivation and emotion. Here, beginning at mid-century, were five really quite different intellectual developments in psychology, each in its own way a rejection (sometimes active, sometimes passive) of the conative and affective.[2]

---

[2]While the case is strong for the neglect by cognitivists of the conative and the affective, I don't want to claim that this was universal—that no vestige of thinking about motivation and, particularly, emotion remained. Indeed there are some notable exceptions, and in the context of one of my major premises, these have come, not surprisingly, not from the animal cognitivists but from those whose work is in human cognition, particularly human memory (see my earlier summary of cognitive subjects, Table 1). Prominent among these is Mandler (e.g., 1984), whose cognitive approach to emotion has been a continuing interest. Another recent example is in the work of Bower and his associates, who, in a series of experiments, have demonstrated again the importance of context, in this case in the form of emotional state-dependency, in memory as well as in a number of other cognitive and semantic processes, such as free-association, selective attention and perception, and selective learning (see Bower, 1981, for a review). Somewhat less in the mainstream, in this respect, was Simon's (1967) brief foray into the motivational and emotional controls of cognition. His approach acknowledged that "motive and emotion are major influences on the course of cognitive behavior [and that] a general theory of thinking and problem solving must incorporate such influences" (p. 29). He then characterized the central nervous system as a serial information processor with requirements for goal-termination and interruption mechanisms, a kind of frustration *ex machina*. The downplaying of the conative and the affective took place, as I have suggested, in a broad-spectrum series of intellectual developments related to a resurging cognitive structuralism. It turned out, however, that the combined force of these various influences toward a pure cognitivism landed more heavily, quite paradoxically, on the animal-cognitive than on the human-cognitive literature out of which it mainly grew.

In the meantime, a psycholinguist, a mathematical learning theorist and a neuropsychologist had combined their efforts to write *Plans and the Structure of Behavior* (Miller, Galanter, & Pribram, 1960), a book and a position that grew in influence from rather modest beginnings to become a rallying point for the new structuralism, which was to become the hallmark of the cognitive government of psychology in the following years. They found another important ally in the unfeeling and unmotivated but all-knowing computer, and in the emerging field of artificial intelligence. It may be of some interest, parenthetically, that this latter field, which started off so structural and so cognitive, now has among its adherents a group that calls itself "connectionists," surely a more functionalist, Thorndikian designation. As Levin (1987) writes in his review of a book on the cognitive revolution in psychology:

> It has been said that cognitive psychology is a disguised S-R formulation with some fancy talk between the S and R. And should the author believe that the history of psychology is linear I would point out that there is discussion again of connectionism among cognitive psychologists, reminiscent of the associationism of behaviorism. (p. 1684)

I take all of this as an example of my favorite physical metaphor for the evolution of theory in psychology, or in any other not-so-highly advanced science: I think of it as a two-dimensional expanding spiral (Fig. 1), a point which moves around a fixed center at increasing distance from that center, coming back to the same spatial orientation each time at an added distance from its origin. The distance—the "facts"—accumulate, but the organizing, orienting principles—the *models*, the *paradigms*—are few, and we periodically come back to those we have previously abandoned. Can anyone really say when we will be out of this epistemological spiral? I suppose the metaphor could be three-dimensional, a conical helix (Fig. 2), and we could think of the third dimension as representing progress.

To come back to theory based on animal learning, there has been, in the words of Thomas S. Kuhn (1962), a "paradigm shift,"

S-R NEOBEHAVIORISM

COGNITIVISM

RADICAL BEHAVIORISM

COGNITIVE NEOBEHAVIORISM

FIG. 1. The expanding spiral. A metaphor for accumulating knowledge and its orienting principles.

but this one so far as I can tell was based not, as Kuhn's thesis requires, on some clear-cut crisis; rather, it would appear to have been influenced by the kinds of factors I have just described, and to have coincided with (and to some extent to have been instigated by) the appearance in 1962 of Kuhn's book, itself. The paradigm shift was based not on any specific identifiable theoretical anomaly, but on a kind of redefinition of psychology, stemming from some general dissatisfaction with the existing definition. The new definition, like a *much* older one, was as the science of the mind; the supplanted definition was as the science of behavior. The result was that the kind of learning theory that was based mainly on animal work began to be treated rather disdainfully, even by those whose subjects were pigeons and rats. These animal cognitivists, who recognized a paradigm shift when they saw one, adopted the language and the models of human cognitive psychology and information processing. Consequently, instead of using animals as models for human function, they were now back to the kind of subjectivism and anthropomorphism the behaviorists had rejected: They were using animal behavior as a vehicle for their introspections, for understanding the mind, much as the artificial intelligence people do so elegantly with computers; and they were using humans as models for animal cognition. This use of humans as models for animals can happen *only in psychology*!

(When I was revising this lecture, and thinking about the influence of Thomas Kuhn, I remembered something my wife pointed out to me. She had been hearing the word paradigm used a lot by friends and colleagues in the behavioral sciences and looked

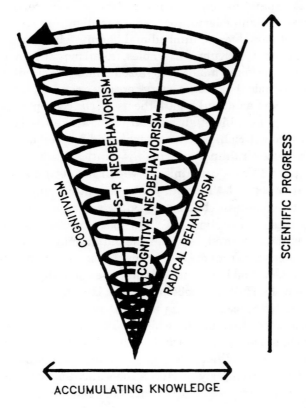

FIG. 2. The three-dimensional conical helix as a metaphor.

it up in a dictionary. She found that "paradigm" was preceded in this dictionary by "paradiddle," and that "paradiddle" is defined as the pattern of a drumbeat, whereas "paradigm" is defined simply as a pattern, and also in most dictionaries, as a model or example. This unexpected piece of intelligence was something I knew I had been looking for ever since Kuhn's book came out a quarter century ago: A metaphor arises for me out of an image that substitutes "paradiddle" for "paradigm" in most cases of its use, at least by those "friends and colleagues in the behavioral sciences." This facile use of "paradigm" does become a drumbeat—a double or even a triple paradiddle, in the words of a song of my youth—to which, happily, we march along thinking we know where we're going. We ought to be more selective about when, in our march along the expanding spiral of my metaphor, a perceived change in direction is dignified with the term "paradigm," in Kuhn's sense, lest we find ourselves benumbed and bemused by "paradiddles." A paradigm shift, in Kuhn's examples, taken mostly from the physical sciences, is some major recognized change in guiding principles and methods that occurs every century or so—not every couple of years, or even months. I regard the use of the concept of paradigm in psychology as a bit of an affectation: It's like the story about the man who got rich, bought a yacht, and arrived at his Jewish mother's house for dinner wearing his nautical garb. "Look at me, ma," he says, "I'm a captain!" To which his doting but worldly-wise mother replied, "By you, you're a captain, and by me, you can also be a captain—but by captains, you're no captain.")

As I pointed out earlier, the "new look," which uses behavior to understand the mind, is not in the old Tolmanian style, which was the other way around: He used mentalistic-sounding constructs to try to understand behavior. Tolman's was actually also the style of Hull and the Hullian neobehaviorists. Hull hid his "cognitive" proclivities by conceptualizing as habit mechanisms terms such as purpose and anticipation—whereas Tolman's signification and expectation stood as they were. I observed some time ago (Amsel, 1962) that the basic difference between most of Tolman and a large part of Hull (particularly in Hull's theoretical papers, see Amsel and Rashotte, 1984) was a difference between a cognitive-expectancy and a conditioning-expectancy language. But both of these systems, Tolman's and Hull's, were behaviorisms, though one was cognitive and the other S-R. It is a fundamental and almost universal confusion nowadays that behaviorism and S-R are taken to be synonyms. What needs to be understood is that behaviorism (or neobehaviorism) is a definition of psychology; S-R, like Tolman's cognitivism, is an approach to theorizing. It is important to understand that a theory is an S-R theory, not because, as some cognitivists insist, it relates the antecedent observable S to the consequent palpable R: *Everyone*, even cognitivists, uses the terms stimulus and response in this way. A theory is an S-R *theory* because, just as cognitive theorists choose to use mental-sounding explanatory constructs, S-R *theorists* choose more physiological-sounding terms and use Ss and Rs to represent the afferent and efferent—and even the central—mediating machinery. A psychology defined as the science of the mind, rather than as a science of behavior, could, in principle, be developed on the basis of mind represented by Ss and Rs, in the same way that Tolman's behaviorism was developed on the basis of mentalistic constructs, such as cognitions, demands, and sign-Gestalt-expectations.[3]

---

[3]Toward the end of a recent essay on "animal awareness," Gordon Burghardt (1985) writes as follows, cryptically and without elaboration:

> [Tolman] is the one American learning theorist respected by classical ethologists, the newer cognitive psychologists, and the animal cognition psychologists. Yet the focus has been on his concepts, not his method. Hull, not Tolman, is the guiding spirit for most cognitive psychologists. (p. 917)

My reading of the recent cognitive literature—and particularly the animal-cognitivist literature—causes me to be skeptical of the first part of this statement. I see little reference in these writings to Tolman's concepts, with the exception of "cognitive map." Tolman was cognitive in his approach to theorizing about the learning factors, but he had also a variety of motivational and organismic constructs in his theories. These, as I have indicated, are notably absent from the recent cognitive formulations of conditioning and learning. The second part, which endows recent cognitive positions with Hull's spiritual guidance, presumably because they employ Hull's methods, I find equally perplexing—unless it is simply that Hull's "methods" are taken to be Pavlovian and Thorndikian/Skinnerian, as for the most part are those of the two branches of animal cognitivism. Hull took experimental support for his theorizing wherever he could find it, and in his *Principles of Be-*

ISSUES AND CONTROVERSIES,
PAST AND PRESENT

In the field of animal learning, which historically has been the arena for competing conceptualizations in learning theory, there were two sets of competing ideas: One major issue has divided the behaviorist, Skinner, and his experimental analysis of behavior, from the neobehaviorists; the others have divided the neobehaviorists, particularly the camps of Tolman and Hull. It may be worth our time to go back and look at these older issues to get some perspective on the ones raised by, and the contributions made by, the animal cognitivists.

The divisions among learning theorists nowadays are between cognitivism and behaviorism. Those among the learning theorists of the 1930s to 1950s were mainly about S-R *theories* and cognitive *theories*; they did not divide behaviorism and cognitive psychology. All of the major theorists in that era were behaviorists, in the spirit of either the earlier or the later Watson. But there were nevertheless five fundamental issues. The first, separating the behaviorist, Skinner, and the neobehaviorists, was methodological: It concerned the relative merit in theorizing of two approaches—the positivistic-inductive and the hypothetico-deductive. The other four related issues, which involved mainly the followers of Tolman and Hull, can be stated as questions: What is learned? How is it learned? Is learning incremental or sudden? Is discrimination learning relational or specific?

As these issues are reviewed, they will be related to recent writings of the animal cognitivists. These theorists have emerged out of two quite different traditions. One of these is the Pavlovian, or perhaps better, the Konorskian. This group of theorists, I believe, was strongly influenced by Konorski's (1967) book, *Integrative Ac-*

---

havior there is an equal-parts blend of the two experimental methodologies. But in the work of the animal cognitivists of learning, these methods are demonstrably not taken from Hull. They are taken directly from Pavlov and Konorski in one case and from Skinner in the other. It is fair to say, moreover, that most of the Skinnerian (or operant) cognitivists, and the younger Pavlovian cognitivists, are not highly schooled in Hull's theorizing or in its experimental basis.

tivity of the Brain, which involved a much more cognitive approach to interpretations of conditioning than Pavlov would have tolerated. There have been various degrees of departure from Konorski's cognitivism in this book, some that have gone far enough to be characterized by the phrase "conditioning is a window on the mind."

The second tradition out of which animal cognitivists have emerged is, surprisingly, the Skinnerian, and amongst other departures from the orthodox position this group of cognitivists seems to have abandoned Skinner's inductive, fact-finding approach for a representational, theoretical one.

Inductive Versus Deductive Approaches

Some years ago, in trying to understand this difference between the hypothetico-deductive approach of Hull's and Tolman's neobehaviorisms and the inductive approach of Skinner's radical behaviorism, I developed an extended metaphor for this difference in approach to theorizing. This was an attempt to express the naive view that the scientist should be more concerned with discovery than with the *form* discovery should take. I offered the opinion that the distinction between inductive and deductive approaches to learning theory had been overdone—too finely drawn from the viewpoint of the scientist; that obviously nobody's theory was all inductive or all deductive; and that, while differences in emphasis existed, these boiled down to differences in the strategy of finding relationships, to differences in the degree to which unifying concepts were sought, and to differences in the temperament of the theorists. The metaphor I employed in my argument was the following one (Amsel, 1965). Remember as you read this long quote that it was written in the late 1950s, for an AAAS symposium on "The Future of Contemporary Learning Theories" in which I was the proponent of the Hull-Spence system, which was under constant attack for its "hypothetico-deductive" orientation—a label that it bore in large part because Hull and others had written a rather emptily formal book entitled *Mathematico-Deductive Theory of Rote Learning* (1940). Anyway, here is my metaphor on inductive versus deductive approaches.

[R]ecall the children's puzzle in which numbered points are joined to form the outline of an object or animal—("find what is hidden by joining the dots") [Fig. 3a]. To see that the hidden thing is a chicken, one joins the dots in numerical order and an outline of the bird emerges [Fig. 3b]. All you have to know to solve this puzzle is (a) the rules of numerical order, and (b) how to draw lines from one point to another. For our purposes, let "point" be an experimental (or other) datum, and let "chicken" be a *pattern* of related experimental (or other) data—a higher-order relationship; an integration of knowledge; a theory. The question: What set of tactics should be followed in the discovery of the chicken? The answer, in the case of the example we have given, is quite simple. Join the points and see what it gets you. The rules are clear and unambiguous; the animal is there to be uncovered; the only thing to hold you up is finding the next numeral.

Now let us change the game a bit. The page is now, not a scattering of isolated dots with numerals next to them, but a page almost black with dots [Fig. 3c]. Only some of these dots outline the pattern which is hidden, and there are no numerals at all to guide the joining of these critical points. But you still have to find the hidden animal, by joining dots. You don't know how many dots to join, or where they are on the page. Your task is complicated by the fact that in order to outline the hidden animal you must first find the points in the total complex of points that are relevant (have a number) and then find what number each point has.

It is in this kind of game that the difference between an inductive and a deductive approach might have some meaning for the scientist. The difference is in the strategy of finding the relevant points, as well as in discovering how each relevant point fits into the pattern, i.e., what number it has. If every point on the page which is black with dots represents a possible experiment to determine if that point is relevant to the outline, one can proceed systematically, for example from left to right and top to bottom, as in reading, to test whether points have numbers or not. If an experiment uncovers a relevant variable, the point achieves some identity; if it does not, the point remains numberless and contributes nothing to the outline one seeks. This is playing the game inductively. However, even with such an inductive approach there comes a time when enough numbers are evident so that the locations of others are suggested [Fig. 3d]. At this stage, the procedure becomes deductive. The player is now reasoning: "If this pattern is in fact the profile of a chicken, as it appears, the other points ought to be about here, and here, and there." . . .

The relatively deductive strategy in psychological theory is only a matter of guessing earlier in the game, and adopting procedures for testing these guesses. The deductively-oriented player is trying to keep from having to test every point (or most of them) on the page. He is trying to find the outline of the hidden animal by doing 100 experiments rather than perhaps 10,000. He reasons that while he may end up having to do just as many as his "inductive-minded" friend, it is unlikely he will have to do any more and, if he is lucky, he may get away doing far fewer. . . .

What I am saying is that at any point in time, the major difference between inductive and deductive approaches to theory-building is the manner of deciding what to look at next; the strategy for deciding what experiment to try. In the terms of our puzzle analogy, the difference is in how to go about finding the relatively few points out of the many which are numbered and which, joined together systematically, will yield a meaningful pattern [Fig. 3e]. (pp. 188-191)[4]

Skinnerians, all of whom were in those days radical behaviorists, are nowadays split on this issue: There are those who still favor the inductive, fact-finding, experimental-analysis-of-behavior approach of post-1950 Skinner; and there are those who can be said to have found at least part of their style of discovery in a more deductive approach—an approach, as we shall see, that involves explanation in terms of intermediary representational constructs. So the issue in learning theory that surrounds inductive versus deductive approaches can no longer be defined as clearly as it was possible to do years ago, as an issue between the Skinnerian behaviorists and the neobehaviorists; and it was never an issue at all *among* neobehaviorists, particularly between followers of Hull and Tolman, whose theoretical disagreements, as we have seen, took the forms of the other four issues I outlined earlier.

What is Learned?

How should conditioning and learning be characterized? Follow-

---

[4]From *Scientific Psychology: Principles and Approaches*, Edited by Benjamin B. Wolman and Ernest Nagel. Copyright © 1965 by Basic Books, Inc., Publishers. Reprinted by permission of the publisher.

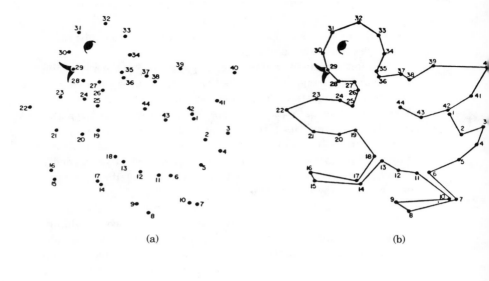

(a)

(b)

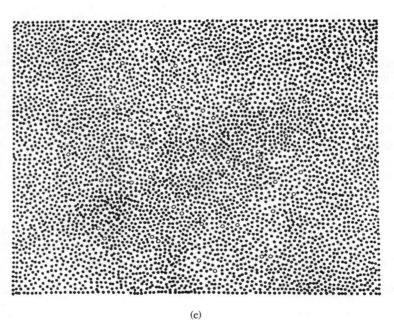

(c)

FIG. 3a-e. The find-the-chicken analogy to inductive versus deductive approaches in science.

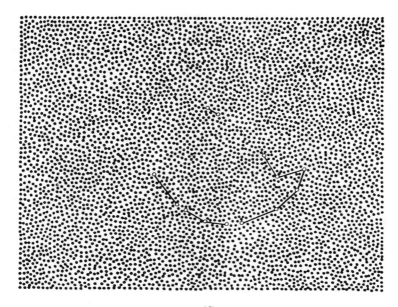

(d)

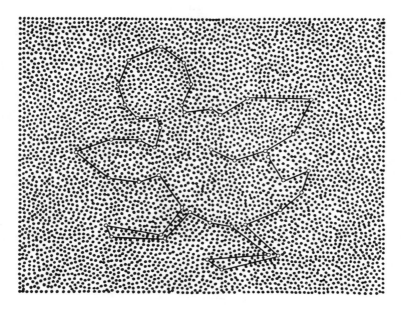

(e)

47

ing Thorndike and Hull, should it be as hypothetical strengths of connections or associations or habits between stimulus and response (S-R)? Following Pavlov, should it be as quasi-physiological central cortical states? Or should it be put in the more cognitive-perceptual terms of Tolman—as relationships between sign and significate (S-S) in classical conditioning, or among sign, behavior and significate (S-B-S) in instrumental learning? This was an issue which, in the 1930s and 1940s, separated the positions of Tolman and Hull and their followers. I represent these positions in Fig. 4, along with Skinner's early position and Kurt Lewin's. Tolman's construct language for what is learned was cognitive: Sign-Gestalt-Expectation, Cognitive Map; Lewin's was physical-mathematical: Field Forces, Valences, Vectors; Hull's was behavioral-physiological: Habit Strength (S_sH_rR), the lower case s and r representing the neural traces of the stimulus and response, Excitatory and Inhibitory Potential, Afferent Neural Interaction. Hull's Anticipatory Goal Response corresponded to Tolman's Sign-Gestalt-Expectation. Guthrie, and later Skinner, favored a more atheoret-

WHAT IS LEARNED?

TOLMAN:

$$\text{SIGN} \rightarrow \boxed{\begin{array}{c}\text{GESTALT-EXPECTATION} \\ \hline \text{COGNITIVE MAP}\end{array}} \rightarrow \text{BEHAVIOR}$$

SKINNER (1938):

$$\text{STIMULUS} \rightarrow \boxed{\text{REFLEX RESERVE}} \rightarrow \text{RESPONSE}$$

LEWIN:

$$\text{SITUATION} \rightarrow \boxed{\begin{array}{c}\text{FIELD FORCES, VALENCES,} \\ \text{VECTORS}\end{array}} \rightarrow \text{BEHAVIOR}$$

HULL:

$$\text{STIMULUS} \rightarrow \boxed{\begin{array}{c}\text{s HABIT STRENGTH } r \\ \text{s-H-r}_g\text{--s}_g\text{-H-r}\end{array}} \rightarrow \text{RESPONSE}$$

FIG. 4. What is learned? The intervening constructs of Tolman, Skinner, Lewin, and Hull.

ical (radical empiricistic) behaviorism, staying as close as possible as often as possible to language of observation. Still, the fact is that all of these learning theorists, even Skinner in his *Behavior of Organisms* (1938), conceptualized intermediary processes between input and output—between environment and behavior—and with the possible exception of Lewin, all were some kind of behaviorist. They were either neobehaviorists, as I have argued, in the sense of the 1913/1919 Watson, or they were followers of Watson's later, more radical departure from the more moderate, functionalist behaviorism with which he started.

In the context of the "What is learned?" question, there is an interesting point to be made about Skinner's behaviorisms before and after the publication of his paper, "Are Theories of Learning Necessary?" (1950). It is not so much a point, I suppose, as it is a conjecture: I refer here particularly to the influence of Skinner's work in relation to Tolman's and Hull's neobehaviorisms, and particularly to Hull's version of stimulus-response learning theory. In the heat of the experimental controversies that issued from the differences between the "Grand Theories" of these neobehaviorists, with their logical-construct approaches to empiricism, Skinner's important early work, particularly his *Behavior of Organisms* (1938), tended to be neglected. Skinner's behaviorism of 1938 did employ empirical constructs of a Sherringtonian variety, but they somehow never got into the game between the followers of Hull and Tolman. In the 1950 paper, Skinner abandoned such constructs. Now, in the heat of the more recent criticisms of the radical empiricism of Skinner by the animal cognitivists, and even by the "liberalized" Skinnerians, the neobehaviorisms of Tolman and Hull have been misunderstood (not to say neglected); and Skinner's early theorizing is still almost never mentioned. What has emerged is a hybrid of the Skinnerian methodology and the recent cognitivist views of animal learning. I refer here, as prominent examples, to the writings of Killeen (1987), of Schwartz and Lacey (1982), and of Terrace (1984). Collectively, these (and others) have moved into position as another version of animal cognitivism, in a sense a new kind of neobehaviorism. This "Emergent Behaviorism," to give it Killeen's designation, reminds one of N. E. Miller's (1959) liberalized Hullianism ("Liberalization of Basic S-R Concepts"). And I think it fair to say that this liberalized, more permissive Skinneri-

an behaviorism is closer to the less extreme (earlier) Watson than
to the more radical (later) Watson; and, to follow my earlier argument, in moving away from Skinner's position it has moved closer
than it used to be to the neobehavioristic theorizing of Tolman (and
even Hull), though this does not seem to be understood by its propo-
nents and adherents.

Here is an example: As a kind of general reply to the "What
is learned?" question, Killeen writes, "We should study behavior,
but we should also study what goes on inside organisms" (p. 225).
As to what goes on inside organisms, Killeen agrees with Zuriff
(1976, p. 51) that: "The decision as to whether to limit psychological theory to stimulus-response relationships . . . or to admit non-
behavioral theoretical terms would seem to depend only on the
heuristic values of the two approaches." These two observers are,
then, in agreement that it is time for followers of Skinner to abandon his rigid prohibition against explanation in terms of empirical constructs. But in the context of this conversion experience,
Killeen writes as though the constructs of Fig. 4, representing
"what goes on inside organisms," the "non-behavioral theoretical
terms" of Zuriff, were not already a part of other behaviorisms.
It has never been debatable—certainly not among neobehaviorists—
that explanations should involve constructs, and that explanatory success (and I would add economy of explanation) should be the
coin of the realm of theories of behavior. And it is really not debatable either that stimulus-response *theory* refers, as it did in
Hull's 21 papers in *Psychological Review* (see Amsel & Rashotte,
1984), as well as in his *Principles of Behavior* (1943), to hypothetical states and processes that "[go] on inside organisms." This being the case, we have come some way toward closing a circle, with
post-1950 Skinner still outside of it. So far as I am aware, this close
correspondence between what Killeen now calls "emergent behaviorism" and the earlier "neobehaviorisms" has not previously
been acknowledged. Indeed, Terrace (1984), another liberalized
Skinnerian, writes that "so-called S-R models rely exclusively on
observable (or potentially observable) stimuli and responses" (p.
8). Perhaps he thinks this because, like others, he has become comfortable with cognitive, representational constructs. The fact is that
for the present S-R theorist, as I think for Hull and certainly for

Spence, the mediating machinery defined as hypothetical Ss and Rs are no more or no less permissible, and no more or no less observable, than are the cognitive constructs the "emergent behaviorists" are now willing to permit, or the "charm" of certain subatomic particles in theoretical physics. It was drummed into those of us whose intellectual upbringing was in the combined traditions of that fundamental Newtonian, Clark Hull, of Tolman's concept of the intervening variable, and of operational definition that to think otherwise was a kind of heresy.

Skinner, himself, is still a strong voice speaking against the cognitivist leanings of the Emergent Behaviorists, as is Dinsmoor (1983), an eminent and more traditional Skinnerian, who, in the context of a stimulus-response analysis of the observing response and conditioned reinforcement, makes the following four points:

1. "Unfortunately for clarity of discourse, the word 'cognitive' seems to have taken on several meanings, which are strongly associated in practice but quite distinct in logical definition" (p. 693). Dinsmoor points out, as I have done in the previous chapter, that cognitive psychology does not refer to a coherent theory but to areas of research—attention, perception, language, memory, imagery and problem solving—that have expanded rapidly as the advent of small computers made them easier to study.

2. Cognitive psychologists of animal learning have been employing Tolman's strategy but not his theoretical structure. By this, I think Dinsmoor means that these psychologists play the role of critics: that instead of establishing a coherent theoretical base, their views can only be understood in terms of the more coherent and established theories they criticize. To paraphrase, in terms of the parliamentary metaphor I have used here and in other places (e.g., Amsel, 1982), these "victorious" revolutionaries continue to act as a "Loyal Opposition" rather than as a "Government."

3. These animal cognitivists claim that "the essence [of their view is] that mediating states or processes are postulated" (Dinsmoor, p. 724), meaning, presumably, that this theoretical strategy of theirs is something new and unprecedented in the history of learning theory. Dinsmoor cites Hull's (1943), and even aspects of Skinner's, theorizing to the contrary. I would go back even to

early Watson (1913, 1919), would cite again Fig. 4, and, as an outstanding example, the earliest writings of Hull in learning theory (see Amsel & Rashotte, 1984).

4. "Some writers seem to use the word 'cognitive' as a weapon of propaganda. The implication is that the person who adopts the label is abreast of the times and that the rest of us, poor souls, are mired in the past. The research we have done was guided by outmoded ideas and may be swept into the dustbin" (Dinsmoor, p. 724). Dinsmoor points out that the word "cognitive" has become a "buzzword" in contemporary psychology, and appears to share my concern that, as a result, a vast store of experimentally derived information is in danger of losing its archival value, at least for a generation of learning theorists.

There is a degree of reassurance in the detailed agreement I find between the views of the behaviorist, Dinsmoor, and my own neobehaviorist position with respect to the cognitive revolution, particularly as it is manifested in the field of animal learning. (In other contexts and respects our positions would, of course, clearly be different.) Our views are undoubtedly shared by others in the field of animal learning who have not been swept up in the fervor of the cognitive conversion.

I have been developing the idea that the "What is learned?" question divided not only the neobehaviorists, Tolman and Hull, but has also recently begun to divide Skinnerians. The other issues in my original list divided the two neobehaviorists. In the form of questions, they were: Is reinforcement a necessary condition for the formation of an association (for learning) rather than just for performance? Do such associations, or expectations in Tolman's sense, gain strength incrementally or do they arise in full strength on a single occasion? Is learning—and particularly discrimination learning—relational or does it proceed by virtue of the accretion of specific excitatory and inhibitory strengths to the positive and the negative stimuli, respectively?

Like the others, these three issues have been around for some time and have had a great deal of play in the form of "crucial" experiments. They represent fundamental and unanswered questions in the psychology of learning and memory, and so, to paraphrase Frost's poem with which we began, it is not surprising that when history is forgotten they can arise again in contexts quite different from the Tolman-Hull debates which featured them. I should like for a moment to go back to them in the context, particularly, of the new Pavlovian animal cognitivism.

How is it Learned?

This question took life in the issue of reinforcement versus contiguity in learning, raised excitement between the supporters of Hull and Tolman, and was argued in the specific context of the latent-learning experiment, in its various forms. (There was no resolution, but it will undoubtedly come at the molecular, neurochemical level, where we may discover there is truth on both sides.) From the perspective of our present analysis of the tenets of the cognitive revolution in animal learning, "How is it learned?" is secondary to the "What is learned?" question, but it comes into its own in the form of the venerable learning-performance distinction. The distinction was accepted and recognized as absolutely crucial in the controversy over latent learning by both Tolman and Hull, and by their followers. But much more important than the latent-learning arguments was the central position of the learning-performance distinction in the formal theories of so many theorists, including these two neobehaviorists. In each of the cases I have presented in Fig. 5, the statements were in the form of general equations, in most cases relating response strength or behavior (performance) as dependent variables to a number of intervening variables, one of which represented learning or cognition, the other(s), one or more of the nonassociative (e.g., motivational) factors. Indeed, Tolman (1938) and Hull (1943, 1952) constructed elaborate conceptual representations of the associative and nonassociative factors controlling behavior. This kind of distinction was also made in other theories (Schachter & Singer, 1962; Simonov, 1969), in which emotion or affect, expressed verbally or in terms of facial expression, rather than a more general category of response or behavior, was the dependent variable. (The learning-performance distinction is not explicit in the writings of Watson

THE LEARNING-PERFORMANCE DISTINCTION

<u>WOODWORTH</u>:   BEHAVIOR = f(MECHANISM, DRIVE)

<u>TOLMAN</u>:   BEHAVIOR = f(COGNITIONS, DEMANDS)

<u>HULL-SPENCE</u>:   RESPONSE STRENGTH = $f[(_SH_R)\,x\,(D + K) - i_R \cdot _SO_R]$

<u>LEWIN</u>:   BEHAVIOR = f(PSYCHOLOGICAL ENVIRONMENT, PERSON)

<u>SCHACHTER</u>:   EMOTION = f(SITUATION AS PERCEIVED x AROUSAL)

<u>SIMONOV</u>:

EMOTION = -NEED (INFORMATION NECESSARY - INFORMATION AVAILABLE)

<u>BINDRA</u>:

RESPONSE = f(SELECTIVE ATTENTION, CENTRAL MOTIVE STATE)

FIG. 5. The learning-performance distinction in the general equations of a number of theorists.

or Guthrie, or in post-1950 Skinner, though it was certainly implicit in Skinner's earlier writings.)

Parenthetically, Fig. 5 is one I could well have employed earlier, in my discussion of the trilogy: cognitive, conative, and affective. My point at the time would have been that, in the wake of the cognitive revolution, nothing to the right of the equals sign except for the first item plays a role in behavior.

In his book, *Contemporary Animal Learning Theory*, Dickinson (1980) makes what he regards as an important distinction between "behavior analysts" and "learning theorists." In the first category he places Hull, Guthrie, Mowrer, and Skinner (there is no reference to Tolman in the book); the inhabitants of the learning-theorist category, though not specified, are identified by the context as Dickinson himself, and presumably the other animal cognitivists mentioned in the book—the most referenced are Mackintosh, Rescorla, and Wagner—whose thinking about Pavlovian conditioning, *spe-*

cifically, includes explanations in terms of representational, memorial processes. Let me say, parenthetically, that Marr (1983) has asserted, and I agree, that "representation is one of the most dominant [concepts] in cognitive psychology and . . . is a key element stimulating the development of cognitive animal psychology . . . " (p. 17). (Representation will be a subject in chapter 3.)

What drives this distinction between "behavior analyst" (a term made synonymous with "behaviorist") and "learning theorist" for Dickinson, and in different terms for others of the same persuasion (see Roitblat, Bever, & Terrace, 1984), is made quite explicit by Dickinson, who, like the "emergent behaviorists," thinks that behaviorists, including neobehaviorists, reject the use of intermediary constructs (see Figs. 4 and 5) and, as a corollary, that they fail to take into account what he calls "behavioral silence," a concept that bears some resemblance to Rescorla's (1980) concept of "detecting learning." Dickinson gives us the following example, amongst others, of the failure of behavior analysts to use explanatory constructs: Behavior analysts, for example Hull and Mowrer, unlike learning theorists, do not use intermediary constructs like fear (as learning theorists do) to describe the effects of exposure to shock; behavior analysts, according to Dickinson, say the animal learns to freeze (p. 4). This remarkable assertion, of course, simply shuts out an important part of the work of the Pavlovian and Hullian neobehaviorists. It is also, of course, entirely incorrect. As a by-product of his participation in Hull's seminars at Yale, Mowrer (1939) wrote what I have always regarded as a landmark paper, entitled "A Stimulus-Response Analysis of Anxiety and Its Role as a Reinforcing Agent." More to the literal point of Dickinson's distinction is another of Mowrer's many papers, "Fear as an Intervening Variable in Avoidance Conditioning" (Mowrer & Lamoreaux, 1946). The conceptualization of fear in avoidance learning by behaviorists and neobehaviorists, in the many papers of N. E. Miller, in the work of R. L. Solomon and his students, and all the way back to Watson and Rayner's (1920) work with Little Albert on the "Conditioned Emotional Reaction," are cases in point. A concept very similar to Watson and Rayner's, as we have seen, is the "Conditioned Emotional Response" of Estes and Skinner

(1941). And, to close this circle, the CER technique is one that is very important to the animal cognitivists, and, as we shall see, provided them with the concept of "surprise" in Pavlovian conditioning.

In this connection, an odd—if not a paradoxical—feature of modern animal cognition is that, unlike Tolman's version, it chooses for its main testing ground two of the simplest kinds of learning: habituation, considered by some to be a kind of psychological "vacuum," and Pavlovian or classical conditioning; whereas, at the same time, it opposes a neobehavioristic S-R tradition which began with the earliest papers in learning theory of Hull, and included the work of Spence, Miller, Mowrer, and others. In these papers, simple conditioning, when it was not studied in its own right, was taken to be a model for internal, including incentive-motivational events in instrumental behavior—it was what came to be known as the two-process approach to theorizing, which, I submit, took its major early form in Hull's r_G-s_G mechanism. So, clearly, if there is a difference between the "behavior analysts" and "learning theorists," it surely does not reside in the use of intermediary constructs or in the level of complexity of the to-be-explained behavior, but rather it lies in the level of complexity of the explanation of the simplest behaviors.

In discussions of the so-called "problem of behavioral silence" (Dickinson, 1980, p. 15), and in Rescorla's indirect detection of learning, there appears to be implicit a claim by the animal cognitivists that one of the advantages of a cognitive approach is in its ability to deal with the fact that learning can occur and its effect(s) not be reflected in behavior. (The "behavioral spade" doesn't always "disinter the thought.") This "behavioral silence" business is another example of attacking radical behaviorism and extending the arguments to behavioristic thinking in general, and neobehaviorism in particular, *where these arguments do not apply*. Had the characterization of all previous learning theorists as "behavior analysts" been restricted to Skinner's later radical empiricism, or even to Skinner and Guthrie, it might have been acceptable; but, as we have seen, it included Hull and Mowrer (and should have included Tolman). The Hull–Spence theory, for example, speaks volubly for behavioral silence (see Fig. 5): If there is no D (or D + K) to multiply H, or if inhibition exceeds excitation, or if behavioral oscillation takes excitatory potential below threshold, then behavior must be silent, regardless of the associative strength (H). And, of course, "behavioral silence" could be found in Hull's (1934) concept of the "habit-family-hierarchy," which can be said to have been anticipated by Watson (1919). According to this concept, learning can be "detected," to use Rescorla's language, only in the case of the dominant habit in the hierarchy in a given situation; all other habits are at that moment "silent."

Is Learning Incremental or Sudden?

It should have become obvious that, in every case, the points raised by the animal cognitivists against behaviorism, S-R psychology, or neobehaviorism had already been subjects for extensive discussion and controversy between behaviorists and neobehaviorists, and between the different schools of neobehaviorism. In some cases the arguments raised by cognitivists straddled several of the "critical" issues of earlier times. We have been discussing one such case, "behavioral silence" or "detecting learning." This was addressed not only in the questions "What is learned?" and "How is it learned?" but also in Spence's (1940) response to the argument, raised by Krechevsky (1938), against continuity in discrimination learning, as well as in the controversy over latent learning. In Spence's (and others') experiments on continuity in learning (see T. S. Kendler, 1971), the trick was to show that the learning of a discrimination was retarded by the prior training on the reverse of that discrimination. It was, however, crucially important to the continuity position that discrimination training in the first (or "presolution") phase be terminated before there was behavioral evidence that any learning had occurred; that is to say, the first-phase learning had to be cut off while it was still "behaviorally silent" for the point of continuity in discrimination learning to be made. (The cognitivists of that day took the opposite position on the issue, by the way.) Spence, of course, was trying to prove that even though, as Krechevsky argued, discriminations appeared to be formed suddenly (insightfully), there was a period of "behavioral silence" preceding solution during which something was being learned—that differential excitatory and inhibitory strengths were accruing to S+ and S−, respectively, and that the difference between these excitatory and inhibitory tendencies had to reach some threshold level before the behavioral silence could be broken. (In the case of latent-learning experiments, on the other hand, Tolman's followers used behavioral silence to argue that reinforcement was not necessary for learning, though it operated as a motivational variable in performance—that the learning would remain latent until appropriately motivated into behavior.)

For more recent examples of "behavioral silence" in neobehaviorism that come readily to mind, I turn briefly to Frustration Theory. As I have indicated, Rescorla (1980) made the point that Pavlovian conditioning can be detected in indirect ways, and not only in its reflexive classical form. Some of the Frustration Theory examples are cases of what I have called mediated generalization (e.g., Amsel, 1967). The evidence is that specific responses (Ross, 1964) or specific response rituals (Rashotte & Amsel, 1968) can be shown to emerge in extinction in situations in which those responses were not seen in acquisition, indeed have never before occurred. What we do in these experiments is to train rats to run slow (actually to take time) in order to get a reward at the end of an alley. To take time they learn idiosyncratic response rituals; and using this device, the rats learn to take up about the right amount of time. About half the time they are slow enough, about half the time a bit too fast; consequently, for the same ritualized response they are sometimes rewarded and sometimes frustrated at the goal. When put into a new situation and rewarded without a time requirement, they run normally and very fast. However, when the fast running in this second situation is extinguished, they revert or regress rather dramatically to the response rituals learned in the first situation. In these cases, the theory says that the mediating action of conditioned frustration, learned in the first situation, is "detected" in extinction in the second situation, even though it was not learned in that second situation. Other examples from neobehaviorism have to do more with the concept of conditioned inhibition in Rescorla's work, as he detects it indirectly through summation and retardation tests (Rescorla, 1969, 1985). Lest this kind of approach be regarded as peculiar to those whom

Dickinson calls "learning theorists" as opposed to "behavior analysts," I would again cite Spence's (1940) work on continuity in discrimination learning as a seminal example of the "retardation test" of conditioned inhibition. My own analyses of prediscrimination effects and "resistance to discrimination" (Amsel, 1962; Amsel & Ward, 1965) can be regarded as more recent, and more generalized, versions of the retardation test.

My purpose in this lecture has been to respond to what I regard as some of the misconceptions in the issues that form the guiding ideas of the "animal cognitivists." These include (a) a failure to distinguish among the various brands of behaviorism and neobehaviorism; (b) a failure to distinguish between neobehaviorism and stimulus-response psychology; (c) a failure to recognize that the learning-performance distinction, critical to both Tolman's and Hull's neobehaviorisms, *requires* that learning be "silent" or be susceptible to indirect "detection"; (d) a failure to recognize that the *essence* of these neobehavioristic theories has always been to "admit of non-behavioral theoretical terms . . . "; and, finally, (e) a failure to understand that such theoretical terms, be they behavioristic or cognitive in the recent sense, be judged less by any surplus meaning they may appear to have, and more by the rigor of their definition and their significance—by their success in organizing that segment of the describable world they set out to organize.

When all of these misconceptions are taken into account, there remains but one essential feature on which neobehaviorism and animal cognitivism can be distinguished. That distinguishing feature boils down to a choice of metatheoretical positions. Indeed it boils down to a difference in the definition of learning theory: Is it, as Tolman, Hull, and others have held, a body of intermediary constructs designed to theorize about behavior? Or is it, as the cognitivists declare, the use of behavior as an indirect (and indifferent) tool for getting at mental structure and function? There is, of course, nothing new about this difference in orienting attitude in psychology. It would, however, seem to be an entirely new development in learning theory.

3

Representational and Non-Representational Levels of Functioning: A Possible Conciliation

> *The history of science, with its manifold skirmishes, revolts, rebellions, and revolutions, is Nature's way of reinstating periodically a law of increasing returns. The new generation comes forward with a new method which, under optimal conditions, will be in harmony with a hitherto inaccessible stratum of reality. But there is no pre-established harmony, and a generation, like a god, may fail. Each revolutionary generation moreover is destined to find that its revolution was an illusion, that its standpoint was only partial and remained circumscribed by a reality that is perhaps transgenerational. . . . No scientific standpoint proves to be valid for more than a chapter of existence, which never yields its plot's entirety. The way of wisdom is to understand how "scientific revolution," in its illusory character, is Nature's method for liberating human energies for scientific progress. Thereby we may secure from the gods their gift of serenity. (p. 361)*
> —L. S. Feuer, *Einstein and the Generation of Science*

This quotation from Feuer (1974) opened the final chapter of a commentary in a book on Hull's theoretical papers (Amsel & Rashotte,

1984). In the concluding paragraph of this commentary, we wrote as follows:

> It is sometimes difficult to separate out of the new, "revolutionary" approaches that which should be rendered unto Hull and that which is owed to others. To rephrase an idea from the opening passage from Feuer, not as many of the revolutionary ideas in the psychology of our generation are as inimical to Hull's as they are said to be, just as not as many of his ideas were independent of those of his precursors as he undoubtedly supposed them to be at times. "The way of wisdom" writes Feuer "is to understand how scientific revolution, in its illusory character, is Nature's method for liberating human energies for scientific progress." The wise, be they cognitive theorists, neo-Darwinian evolutionists, or whatever, will recognize that what Hull did and tried to do, what he borrowed and what he added, is part of their heritage. (p. 507)

The second of these quoted passages refers to Hull, but it, along with the words from Feuer, could as easily apply to any of the other leading neobehaviorist learning theorists as to Hull; or to behaviorists like Skinner and Watson. It could, indeed, apply to any of the major theorists in our field. As I develop the topic of this final chapter, representational and non-representational explanations of behavior, I will try to live up to the conciliatory tone of these opening quotations, and in Feuer's words "secure from the gods their gift of serenity," but you may judge that I do not always succeed.

In chapter 2, we saw that "representation" is clearly the most dominant concept in cognitive psychology, and that this can be said of cognitive *animal* psychology as well. I have referred earlier to the fact that, with few exceptions, recent published discussions of the role of cognitive or representational processes in animal learning appear always to revolve about support for, or opposition to, Skinner's behaviorism (e.g., Lloyd, 1986; Marr, 1983; Moore, 1983), and exclude reference to the conceptualizations of the neobehaviorist learning theorists. If one target must be selected, Skinner is of course the easy one because, as recently as this year (Skinner, 1987a, 1987b), he has written on "cognitive thought" and on "a science of feeling" in terms of the "Analysis of Behavior";

indeed, as in the past (e.g., Skinner, 1977), he continues to exclude all and any hypothetical mediating mechanisms from his behavioral analysis. Whether or not this stance of restricting criticisms to Skinner is an intentional strategy of the cognitivists, be they Pavlovian or operant cognitivists, it is difficult to say: Is it simply that a better case can be made against a radical behaviorism than against neobehaviorism? Is it that neobehaviorist views are regarded as unimportant in the contemporary arena, or even in historical perspective? Or, I hesitate to ask, is it strategic forgetfulness? In these lectures I have taken the opportunity to discuss this unbalanced treatment, and I have done so out of a conviction that the neobehaviorist point-of-view should not be ignored or neglected—that it is important. By my reckoning, it is time for the animal cognitivists to go beyond making their easiest case and preaching to the already saved, and to enter into a genuine dialogue with neobehaviorists. In the absence of such an opportunity, I have been presenting my own version of such a dialogue, in an attempt to bring the weights of neobehaviorism and cognitivism into reasonable balance.

Since internal representations do indeed seem to be the stuff of which animal cognition is made, I would like now to provide a version of the history of the concept of "representation" in animal learning theory, and to ask along the way in what sense(s) this concept differs from—and (more important) in what sense it adds to—neobehavioristic accounts of hypothetical intermediary processes. In what sense do cognitive concepts, such as "representation," increase the integrating power of our theories of animal learning, or make them better models for the aspects of human functioning to which they best apply? But before I do this, I would like to get something out of the way—to say something about what has often been regarded as the "first shot" fired in the revolution of the animal cognitivists.

Bolles (1975, p. 249), who I would characterize as a Pavlovian cognitivist, appears to say that "the revolution" (against "traditional learning theory") was touched off by the findings of long-delay learning and of cues-to-consequences relationships in the original work on taste-aversion learning by Garcia and Koelling (1966). Terrace (1984, p. 11), an operant cognitivist, seems also to

regard this work as a factor in the abandonment of the S-R behavioristic paradigm in favor of the animal-cognition approach. (It
is, incidentally, never made clear how Garcia's interesting phenomena are better explained in terms of animal cognitivism.) In
my opinion, these and other very important discoveries, which have
been summarized by the unfortunate phrase, "constraints on learning," are quite orthogonal to the dimension on which behavioristic and cognitive explanations for learning, animal or human, can
be found. Garcia's work on "selective association" cannot be said
to *require* a cognitive interpretation; indeed this exact term, "selective association," was used years ago by neobehaviorists (H. H.
Kendler, 1946; Amsel, 1949) to conceptualize the difference in as-
sociability between relevant and irrelevant drive stimuli, or
"dominant" and "alien" drive stimuli, as Hull (1943) called them.
The property of gustatory stimuli to enter into associative relationship with illness (an "S-R" association, incidentally), even after a very long interval between those CSs and that illness, is still
in some dispute (Bitterman, 1975, 1976; Garcia, Hankins, & Rusiniak, 1976). It was this property that was taken by cognitivists
to be a strong exception to the principle of contiguity in conditioning and learning, and to depend on the particular sensory and motor systems that were involved.

I will now argue that there is some difference between the
factors which moved Pavlovian neobehaviorists like Bolles and
Dickinson toward animal cognitivism, and those which moved
traditional behaviorists like Killeen and Terrace toward animal
cognitivism, and that in both cases Garcia's classic work must be
regarded as a side issue.

WHY DID PAVLOVIAN NEOBEHAVIORISTS
BECOME COGNITIVISTS?

My own view is that the first two shots in the revolution that led
Pavlovian neobehaviorists toward animal cognitivism were fired
in the context of a bandwagon effect—that they were prepared by
the factors, to which I referred in an earlier lecture, that contributed to the cognitive revolution in general. Of these two additional

factors from the animal work, one was general and "inspirational," the other quite specific. The general factor, to which I have already alluded, was the publication in 1967 of Konorski's *Integrative Activity of the Brain*. In this book, Konorski, unlike his mentor, Pavlov, theorized about action of the brain not only in neurophysiological but also in cognitive terms—terms which were quasi-Tolmanian in character. The second, more specific factor in the rebirth of animal cognitivism was Kamin's (e.g., 1968, 1969) use of the word "surprise" to characterize the action of the unconditioned stimulus, particularly, as we shall see, in the phenomenon in Pavlovian conditioning called "blocking." According to Kamin, as an unconditioned stimulus (US) is repeated successively in conjunction with a conditioned stimulus (CS), the US loses its capacity to "surprise," and this reduces its capacity to enter into association with the same or with other CSs on later trials. The idea was that it was the surprising quality of a US that gave it its reinforcing power. This, along with Rescorla's (1967) still-controversial view that "predictability" or "contingency," to the exclusion of simple "pairing" of CS and US, was the critical factor in Pavlovian associative learning, set the stage for the very influential Rescorla-Wagner (1972) model of Pavlovian conditioning and the later and separate writings of Rescorla and of Wagner that stressed the importance of representational processes in the kinds of learning we had always regarded as our most simple: habituation and Pavlovian conditioning.[1]

The Rescorla-Wagner difference equations comprised a model of associative learning not very different in substance from aspects of Hull's equations (1943), and almost identical in form to Bush and Mosteller's (1951) equations. The unique feature of their model, however, was that it provided an associative interpretation of the "attentional" phenomenon of blocking. The adoption by these theorists of the surplus meaning of "surprise" for the action of the

---

[1] A recent book, *An Introduction to Animal Cognition* (Pearce, 1987), appears to be the first textbook in cognitive animal learning. Aside from references to the author himself, the most frequent page references are to Mackintosh, Rescorla, and Wagner. Konorski is referenced twice as often as Pavlov. There are two references to Tolman and two to Hull's books—but none to Hull's papers, which are so much more relevant to "cognition" than are the books.

US produced an intellectual atmosphere in which, for example, Rescorla (1972) would theorize in such terms as "informational variables" and argue for a "cognitive perspective" in Pavlovian conditioning (Rescorla, 1978), and Wagner (1976) would theorize about "expected" and "surprising" events, "information processing," "rehearsal," and "self-generated priming" in habituation and Pavlovian conditioning, and about "expectancies" and "priming" in short-term memory (Wagner, 1978). In all cases, representations of the CS, the US, or both were involved. So, in my opinion, in the Rescorla-Wagner model we see the beginning of a paradox: A theory of simple associative learning, defined by mathematical equations, was the engine, fueled by Kamin's earlier work on blocking and its conceptualization in terms of "surprisingness," that drove the cognitive movement in animal-learning research against its neobehaviorist antecedents—against the Pavlovian neobehaviorism of R. L. Solomon, in Rescorla's case, and against Hull-Spence neobehaviorism in Wagner's case.

We should now ask, "What is the learning-theory meaning of the concept of 'surprise,' and how is it related to—and what does it add to—previous conceptualizations of the action of the unconditioned stimulus?" All learning curves, like most biological growth functions, are negatively accelerated—that is to say, they describe a law of diminishing returns. Most learning theorists adopt a strategy to accommodate this reality; but the strategies can differ, as can the equations which express them. Starting with Thurstone's (1919) learning-curve equation, each mathematical description of learning has had a parameter governing declining increments of growth, and each has had a factor representing some, usually hypothetical, asymptotic value. Even theorists who have believed in, or whose strategies have in some sense required, "one-trial learning" (e.g., Guthrie, 1935; Estes, 1950) have had to adopt mechanisms to account for incremental growth in terms of the accretion of discrete, elemental units learned in a single trial. In theories that have dealt with incremental growth either of response probability (e.g., Bush & Mosteller, 1951) or associative strength (e.g., Hull, 1943; Rescorla & Wagner, 1972), growth to asymptote is specifically depicted in equations. In the earliest of these, Hull's

HULL (1943) -- EXPONENTIAL EQUATION FOR HABIT

$$_SH_R \ - \ M \ - \ Me^{-iN}$$

$_SH_R$	=	value of habit on trial N
M	=	maximum value of habit strength
e	=	empirical constant
i	=	parameter for growth of habit
N	=	number of reinforcements already given

FIG. 6. Hull's exponential equation for habit. When $Me^{-iN} = 0$, the "surprise" is gone.

case, represented in Fig. 6, the equation is

$$_SH_R = M - Me^{-iN}$$

where i is the parameter representing rate of growth and M is the asymptotic value to which H advances. In every case the increments (in our example of $_SH_R$) become smaller and smaller as N (the number of trials) grows larger. The value of i presumably differs from one kind of learning and one species of animal to another. The two other kinds of equations, the one of Bush and Mosteller for response probability, the other of Rescorla and Wagner for associative strength, are represented in Figs. 7 and 8 respectively.

BUSH & MOSTELLER (1951)—LINEAR EQUATIONS
FOR RESPONSE PROBABILITY

$$\Delta p_n = \beta(\lambda - p_n)$$

and

$$p(n + 1) = p_n + \Delta p_n$$

β	=	rate parameter for growth of probability
λ	=	asymptote or limit of probability = 1
Δp_n	=	increment in response probability; a function of already-existing probability p_n

FIG. 7. Bush and Mosteller's linear equations for response probability. When $\lambda = p_n$, the "surprise" is gone.

RESCORLA & WAGNER (1972) -- LINEAR EQUATIONS
FOR ASSOCIATIVE STRENGTH

$$\Delta V_A = \alpha_A \beta_1 (\lambda_1 - V_{AX})$$

$$\Delta V_X = \alpha_X \beta_1 (\lambda_1 - V_{AX})$$

V_A = associative strength of CS_A to the US_1

α_A = stimulus salience of CS_A

β_1 = strength of US_1

λ_1 = asymptote of associative strength that US_1 can support

V_{AX} = associative strength of compound formed by CS_A and $CS_X = V_A + V_X$

$(\lambda_1 - V_{AX})$ = "surprisingness" of US

FIG. 8   Rescorla and Wagner's linear equations for associative strength. When $\lambda_1 = V_{AX}$, the surprise is gone.

In these two cases the equations are of the linear-operator form, though the second one, the Rescorla-Wagner case, requires difference equations because it is a model for stimuli in compound. In both cases, the parenthetical term defines growth to asymptote, in one case of p_n, in the other of V_{AX}. In the Rescorla-Wagner model, to get back to and be specific about the concept of surprise, as the associative strength, V_{AX}, of the compound stimulus, AX, approaches the asymptote, λ_1, the level of surprisingness of the US approaches zero, as do the sizes of the increments in associative strength, ΔV_A and ΔV_X, that can occur.

The rate parameter (i or β) in the case of Kamin's US, electric shock, is very large: Depending on the shock level, it is often difficult to detect further increases in behavioral indicants of conditioned fear after two or three CS-US pairings. The term "blocking" refers to the fact that following a small number of such trials in which (say) a noise (CS A) is paired with shock, very little associative strength accrues to (say) a light (CS X) in a noise/light compound because, presumably, the shock US is no longer "surprising." In appetitive conditioning the rate parameter is much smaller, which means the US stays "surprising" much longer, which in itself seems paradoxical if not surprising. In any event, a word, "surprise," has now been substituted for a parameter in learning equations. I see this substitution not as theory but as metaphor; but this was *some* metaphor in the sociohistory of animal cognition! If the rat or pigeon is surprised, it will "rehearse" the surprising event (the shock or the food) to keep it in short-term memory store long enough to be encoded in long-term memory; if encoded, the memory can be "retrieved"; if this memory is "primed," then the event will not be so surprising next time; if it is not so surprising next time, it will not be so effective in relation to other conditioned stimuli; and if it is not so effective, then the action of CSs in compound can be accounted for. This is a cognitive rendering of the essence of the excitatory aspects of the Rescorla-Wagner model, which in itself can do nicely without any cognitive metaphorical overtones: The model is the formal mathematical statements. It was not so much in this model but, as I have claimed, in their later and separate work that these theorists, following Konorski and Kamin, appear to me to have been the guiding influences in the move toward animal cognitivism, as it came to be practiced by lapsed neobehaviorists. (As we shall see, this work also influenced slipping Skinnerians.) The rebuilding of the inner world of the rat and pigeon in terms of representational structures (more specific than Tolman's "cognitive maps," I suppose because they represent simpler learning) has since followed an accelerating course.

Let me summarize: We have dealt with the origins, as I see them, of a tendency by former neobehaviorists to conceptualize learning in animals, mainly in the laboratory rat, in terms of cognitive, representational processes. My reading of this movement is that it started in the mid-1960s, greatly influenced by the atmosphere created by the earlier rise of a general neo-structuralism, to which I have already alluded in some detail, and was abetted, specifically, by a series of events in animal-learning research, prominent among which were a book by Konorski (1967) and experiments and theory in habituation and in Pavlovian conditioning—mainly indirect Pavlovian conditioning—the thrust of which was to add cognitive complexity to experimental paradigms that psychologists had always held to be their simplest and next-to-simplest.

WHY DID RADICAL BEHAVIORISTS BECOME
COGNITIVISTS?

In a recent issue of *Times Literary Supplement*, B. F. Skinner (1987a) wrote as follows:

> For at least 3,000 years, . . . philosophers, joined recently by psychologists, have looked within themselves for the cause of their behaviour. For reasons which are becoming clear, they have never agreed upon what they have found. Physiologists, and especially neurologists, look at the same body in a different and potentially successful way, but even when they have seen it more clearly, they will not have seen initiating causes of behaviour. What they will see must in turn be explained either by ethologists, who look for explanations in the evolution of the species, or by behaviour analysts, who look at the histories of individuals. The inspection or introspection of one's own body is a kind of behaviour that needs to be analysed, but as the source of data for a science it is largely of historical interest only. (p. 5)

As we have seen, a "liberalization" similar to the Pavlovian cognitivists' emerged about a decade later out of Skinnerian operant ranks, clearly without the blessing of its leader (Skinner, 1977). These radical-behaviorist Skinnerians, formerly dissatisfied with and even scornful of the "spooky" hypothetical-construct theorizing of the neobehaviorists, found cognitive representational constructs much more to their liking. The "animal cognition" movement of Skinnerian behaviorists also occurred in the context of the general atmosphere of the cognitive revolution in psychology, but it came a bit later, and its origins are somewhat more difficult to pinpoint.

What was it that (to use an ethological term) released the cognitive proclivities of these "Experimental Analysts of Behavior" with respect to the explanation of the behavior of that receptacle for knowledge, the pigeon? They were obviously affected to some extent by the same general factors from the "cognitive revolution" that influenced the Pavlovians. But the major releasing stimuli seem to me to have occurred later, in the work of Herrnstein, perhaps Skinner's foremost disciple, on the pigeon's learning of con-

cepts and categories (Herrnstein, Loveland, & Cable, 1976; Herrnstein & De Villiers, 1980; see also Zentall & Hogan, 1976), and
in the work of other Skinnerians on short-term or "working"
memory (Honig, 1978; Shimp, 1976). (The book on "Animal Awareness" by Griffin [1976] appeared at about the same time.) In any
event, what was a trickle in the mid-1970s has become a flood of
animal cognitivism—perhaps a term I used earlier, "operant cognitivism," fits this case better—in the mid-1980s in the metatheory
and the explanatory language of the formerly orthodox Skinnerian behaviorists. The pigeon, previously regarded as a finely-tuned
visual machine, sensitive to reinforcement contingencies, was now
endowed by Shimp not only with knowledge but with "metaknowledge" (Shimp, 1982), and not only with behavior but with
"self-report" of that behavior (Shimp, 1983). That is to say, the
pigeon had not only knowledge, but knowledge about that
knowledge; and not only behavior, but self-awareness of that behavior.[2]

The introductory chapter of the book *Animal Cognition* (Roitblat, Bever, & Terrace, 1984) is a kind of "keynote address" of operant cognitivism. In it, Terrace, like Pavlovian cognitivists before
him, refers to "S-R *models* [as relying] exclusively on observable
(or potentially observable) stimuli and responses" and claims this
is the weakness of "so-called S-R *models* of animal behavior" (pp.
8, 10, italics added). First of all, it is an essential contradiction to
refer to models of observables; and, as I indicated earlier, such
a characterization of S-R models does not fit the neobehaviorism
of Hull, Spence, Miller, or Mowrer—or of any other version of neobehaviorism, including my own. Terrace thinks that representations cannot be characterized as internal responses. The reaction
of a neobehaviorist might be that these representations have to

---

[2]In a recent Research News item in *Science*, "Do Animals Read Minds, Tell
Lies?" (Lewin, 4 December 1987, p. 1350), we are told that chimpanzees and oran-
gutans "appear to have the concept of self" (p. 1351), but that lower primates like
baboons and bushbabies show no evidence of self consciousness. If pigeons have
metaknowledge and self-report, and bushbabies do not, we would be faced with an
extreme example of "Evolution as Tinkering" (Jacob, 1977, p. 1164) in the case
of cognitive representational processes: The Tinkerer, in this case, must have forgotten what He/She had succeeded in putting together millennia—eons—earlier.

be responses *in some sense*; they do not simply float up into consciousness. Consciousness is not, however, a problem for Terrace,
who claims that objections to animal cognition as mentalism are
no longer relevant because cognitive processes are "unconscious"
(p. 7). Although cognitive psychologists who study people imply un-
consciousness in mechanisms underlying subliminal perception,
hypnosis, and the like (see a recent review by Kihlstrom, 1987),
the reaction of a behaviorist might be that unconscious cognition
is not only an etymological contradiction, but is going too far in
the case of pigeons. Be that as it may, this position of Terrace's
is a striking and novel combination of cognitive concepts, Freud-
ian theory, and Skinnerian investigative technique. Another of Terrace's assertions is that the form of the representation, "is immate-
rial . . . as to whether [it] is of the CS, the US, the UR, or of some
S-S or S-R connection" (p. 13). The important thing for him is that
"some type of representation exists." I find such statements, coming from a Skinnerian turned animal cognitivist, as disturbing as
Hull found comparable ones coming from mentalists and Gestalt
psychologists over a half-century ago. It should be as difficult now
as it was then to take seriously a scientific theory whose mechanisms depend so little on contact with the external world.

Terrace also asserts that "the concept of representation [in
animals] should not raise the spectre of dualism . . . [because], as
studies of human cognitive psychology have made clear, it is
meaningful and essential to investigate representations as *psychological* phenomena in their own right" (p. 19). Even leaving aside
this characterization of representations as phenomena, not everyone would agree with either part of this assertion, any more than
Terrace and others, in their days as orthodox Skinnerians, agreed
with the use of Hull's r_Gs or Tolman's expectancies. One could argue that the concept of anticipatory goal response in the various
forms it takes, for example in Frustration Theory, is a generic term
denoting various alternative "representations" of the outcomes of
behavior: "Memory of the goal event" or "goal expectation" are
reasonable translations of r_G. The advantages to me of *this* kind
of "representational" model, however, as I have often pointed out
(e.g., Amsel, 1962), is that it is constrained by specifiable mechanisms—the mechanisms of classical Pavlovian conditioning that

apply in a given context, for given kinds of CS and US, in a given animal, at a given age. The trouble with cognitive representation is that no such set of constraining mechanisms are yet provided, nor perhaps can they be. In the final analysis, the mechanisms of cognitive representation, not only in humans but in rats and pigeons as well, are more subject to being derived from *introspection*, and this can be said as much of the constructs of the "liberalized" or "emergent" Skinnerians as it can of the constructs of the Pavlovian cognitivists. It therefore seems impossible, contrary to Terrace's hopes, not "to raise the spectre of dualism." It was obviously the difficulties raised by dualism in biobehavioral science that caused Hull (1930, 1931) to find in hypothetical conditioned responses and their feedback stimulation, concepts derived from Pavlovian conditioning, a manner of imposing some constraint on theorizing about a class of mechanisms that mediate behavior.

I am reminded of a favorite story told to me by my father, who came to America as an adolescent from Poland. I'm sure it was told to him by his father, and I have told it to my sons (I have no daughters). The story—a parable, almost, in my thinking—is about two friends in a shtetl, I'll call it Duniev, both trying to eke out a living as peddlers. One day, Yossel had to go to a neighboring shtetl, Nuriev, to look into buying some merchandise. He asked his friend, Tevye, who had no business to do that day, to accompany him. They hitched up Yossel's old horse to a wagon and started the journey. Before long there was a steep upgrade in the road and Yossel said to Tevye, "Why don't we get out and walk? The poor horse is old, and we should save its strength for the return trip." They got out and walked. Next, of course, there was a downgrade, and Yossel said, "Since downhill is easy to walk, why should our weight push against the poor old horse?" So they walked downhill. It was uphill and downhill all the way from Duniev to Nuriev and, of course, all the way back, so, apart from getting up and down from the wagon, the friends walked most of the way. When they returned to Duniev, Tevye addressed his friend Yossel as follows: "Yossel," he said, "You had to go to Nuriev to look into the possibility of buying merchandise; this I can understand. I, being a good friend of yours, agreed to go along to keep you company; this I was happy to do. What I can't understand is, why did we have to drag along the poor old horse?"

I take this to be a story of complication by excess baggage. In the context of psychobiological theorizing, the story is an allegorical tale of parsimony. I find it particularly apt in boiling down to its essence the role of cognitive, representational concepts, and terms borrowed from the language of human information processing (the poor old horse), in the explanations we have been offered of the *very simplest kinds of associative mechanisms* with which we deal: sensitization, habituation, conditioning.

By now, for example, you know how a neobehaviorist would answer the following questions: Is the term, "CS representation," used with more theoretical and neurophysiological justification than the more neutral term, "stimulus trace," to account for the perseverating qualities of the CS in, say, trace conditioning? And is the term, "surprisingness" a more advanced scientific descriptor on any given trial of the residual associative potential of the CS, as it relates to the residual reinforcing power of the US, than is a parameter representing the discrepancy between asymptotic and existing values of conditionability? In the case of the second question, molecular evidence for this kind of general mathematical statement (but not, I think, for "surprise") may turn up in recent cellular investigations of levels of presynaptic facilitation in simple invertebrate systems (e. g., Carew, Abrams, Hawkins, & Kandel, 1984).

In a recent paper, Lloyd (1986) expresses the contrary view, and sees no limit to what he calls "cognitive liberalism." On the basis of work on classical-conditioning in Hermissenda (e.g., Alkon, 1974), he ascribes "inner representations" to this and other marine invertebrates, and he rejects Fodor's (1986) somewhat more cautious position that there may be limits to such liberalism: Fodor doesn't think, for example, that paramecia have inner representations. (Paramecia do appear to give evidence of associative learning [Hennessey, Rucker, & McDiarmid, 1979].) Lloyd's position is that representational explanation is to be preferred to both behaviorist and neurophysiological explanations because it "is potentially more comprehensive than its rivals and [because] representations are useful posits wherever internal information-bearing states

mediate behavior" (p. 1). Disregarding for a moment the circulari-
ty of this conclusion, the question for a philosopher (like Lloyd)
may be, How far can cognitive liberalism be taken, in principle?
He thinks that the marine invertebrates—*Hermissenda, Aplysia,
Limax*—that have become the preferred model systems for studying the neurophysiology and neurochemistry of basic conditioning
"can offer heuristic and suggestive model systems in representational psychology . . ." (p. 12). The question for a working biobehavioral scientist is, "Of what real heuristic value is it to extend
the cognitive metaphor to its logical limit?" The point is that, as
this limit is approached, simple S-R connectionist analysis, and the
specific neurophysiology that can be shown to be correlated with
that analysis, do all the explanatory work that is necessary. So,
again, why drag the poor old horse along?

Why is it so out of fashion these days to adopt the more conser-
vative, neobehavioristic rather than the cognitive conceptualization, even in the case of adaptability in the simplest and
next-to-simplest biological systems? Why, even at this level of analysis, does it make people uncomfortable to be called behaviorists
or neobehaviorists? Is it, as Dinsmoor (1983) writes, because it iden-
tifies the *former* behaviorist (or neobehaviorist) converted to cognitivism as enlightened, and the rest of us as "poor souls . . . mired
in the past" (p. 724)? There has to be a better reason for the conversion, even to these extremes of cognitivism, but for some of us
this has been difficult to find.

As learning theorists, we are not yet in a position to discard as
outmoded research and ideas that are really quite recent, as these
things go, and to treat the best minds in the immediate past-history
of our science with not much more than toleration—like familiar
but somewhat senile distant relatives. The danger is that in the
excitement of the new "paradigm," and in our haste to discard the
existing ones, we forget that, in animal learning at least, a case
can be made that theory based on an S-R conditioning model is
tighter, more parsimonious—more constraining—than the cogni-
tive-representational models in the instances in which both are applied to the same phenomena; that the range of phenomena studied
by the S-R neobehaviorists is broader; and that it includes variables that affect motivation as well as association.

The animal-cognitivist approach has a feature that is to my mind unique among the biological sciences: It seems at times to be an animal model of human function, and at other times a human model of animal function. From all that can be gleaned from the literature, I would have to say that (so far, at least) the direction of the major thrust appears to be from the human to the animal work—borrowing concepts, mainly from the work in human memory, to account for cognitive function in animals. Even if it were possible to defend these concepts against charges of anthropomorphism and introspectionism in the human work, it would seem more difficult to do so in the case of rats, pigeons, and at times even the marine invertebrates.

ONTOGENY AND PHYLOGENY AND LEVELS OF FUNCTIONING

In the first half of this chapter, as in the last part of the previous one—indeed, throughout this book—I have been at particular pains to quote from the writings of some of the leading cognitivists, and particularly the animal cognitivists. And in this latter category, I have included representatives of those I have called Pavlovian cognitivists and Skinnerian or operant cognitivists. I have done this because I don't want to be accused of "baying at the moon": I have been responding to some examples of the kind of intellectual attack that has for about twenty years characterized the supporters of animal cognitivism against "Traditional Learning Theory," "Behaviorism," and "S-R Psychology," without very much response. In this same spirit, I want now to conclude by saying something about my own position.

My own strategy is, and has been, to regard the work in classical conditioning as a model for incentive motivation or expectancy in both animals and humans; to consider that there is a level of functioning in sea slugs, rats and people at which learning is incidental or "unintentional"—that is to say, does not already involve representational processes—and that, at certain ontogenetic and phylogenetic levels, this non-representational learning is the dominant and, in some cases, the only kind that occurs. This strategy may not, in the long run, correspond to the whole "truth" of the matter, but I regard it as an effective guiding principle for the present, at least, and I want now to show how something like this kind of approach has been involved in recent and not-so-recent thinking in a variety of quarters. I would like it if, in these last remarks, my stance were taken as even-handed (to mix a limb-ic metaphor)—taking a little from the "lower" levels of function-ing and giving a little to the "higher" ones. And this leads me to a consideration of the ontogeny and phylogeny of such matters.

I begin these last remarks with a quote from D. O. Hebb's, *Essays on Mind* (1980):

> The argument [can be made] that the behavioral signs of mind and consciousness are evident only in the mammals, with the possible exception of some of the larger-brained birds; that relatively small-brained mammals like the rat or the hamster may have very small minds (like the penguins of Anatole France's Penguin Island, to whom the Lord gave souls but of a smaller size)—but still minds, whereas fish and reptiles, and most birds, seem to be reflexively programmed and give little evidence of that inner control to which the term mind refers. The best evidence of continuity, in the develop-ment from lower to higher mammals, is to be found not only in their intellectual attainments, their capacities for learning and solving problems, but also in their motivations and emotions. Man is evi-dently the most intelligent animal but also, it seems, the most emo-tional. (p. 47)

One of the interesting aspects of the work of the animal-cognitivist learning theorists is that, so far as I am aware, it is based almost entirely on the "idealized" *adult* rat and pigeon, and to a lesser extent the rabbit and monkey, and yet the representa-tional cognitive language it has generated appears to have none of the explicit ontogenetic or phylogenetic boundaries which Hebb's observation implies. If it is reasonable to refer to "representations" (conscious or unconscious) in the "very small mind" of the adult rat, and even in the smaller one of the adult pigeon, is it reason-able in decorticate, decerebrate, and even spinal animals? Is it reasonable in the hydranencephalic human infant; in the one-day-old infant rat; in *Aplysia, Hermissenda, Limax* and other invertebrates; in the honeybee; in the *Drosophila* larva; and *reductio ad absurdum*, in *Paramecia* and bacteria? All of these can be said to have a form of memory. In most of these "preparations, " and in many others, something operationally indistinguishable from direct or indirect associative classical conditioning has been observed. The dimensions covered in these examples are the phylogenetic, the ontogenetic, and the non-intact to intact. I pointed out some years ago (Amsel, 1972) that it is essential that we identify a level of associative learning in which mediating, representational processes are not already involved. From a strictly logical point of view, there has to be such a level of association because otherwise it is not possible to conceive of how the expectancies, anticipations, and memories that make up the representations, which make possible the "surprises," can themselves be formed. To accommodate such a logical requirement we must invent—if we don't have it—a fundamental, unmediated ("reflexive," to use Hebb's term) level of associative learning. This brings us to a discussion of levels of associative functioning. Thinking in these terms has made sense to me and, apparently, to Hebb and, as we shall see, to others.

My position is not dissimilar, though it is expressed in more extreme terms and with more extreme examples, to one taken by Estes (1975b) in his introductory "State of the Field" chapter in the first of his five-volume series, *Handbook of Learning and Cognitive Processes*. This statement from the editor of this series stands out in sharp relief against the hardened cognitive positions of Bower, in the chapter that follows Estes' introduction, and of Bolles in the closing chapter of this first volume:

> The basic reason why we not only should but must be multidisciplinary is that the evolution of the human organism has presented us with a fantastically multilayered system, with old and new portions of the brain, more primitive and more sophisticated learning and behavioral mechanisms all existing and functioning side by side—sometimes in almost total independence, sometimes in interactions. Some of the bodily processes of even the most sophisticated human learner are modified by conditioning in accord with laws that

seem indistinguishable from those governing conditioning in lower organisms. In other instances the conditioning processes become overlaid or modulated by verbal and symbolic processes in ways so complex as almost to defy analysis. In some instances the behavioral subsystem that is undergoing conditioning may be sufficiently isolated as to be conveniently ignored by the investigator of verbal or symbolic activities. In other instances, conditioning processes are inextricably involved in the development of emotions, motivations, or attitudes that are most relevant to the way in which the individual's cognitive state influences his behavior.

At the same time, one should not view mechanisms of conditioning and reinforcement solely in terms of their bearing on vegetative and motivational functions, which are largely obscured in the more cognitive activities of the adult human being. Of necessity, research on conditioning in lower organisms has sometimes led into periods of refined and exacting analysis of the manner in which particular response systems are modified, yielding results that can only be interpreted by a few specialists. Nonetheless, research on conditioning in the same organisms, and in fact sometimes in the same experiments, bears on the processes and mechanisms by which animals gain information about their environments. On the surface, these processes are quite remote from those we observe in the adult human being, but for understanding both lower and higher organisms the similarities may be more significant than the differences. Principles of operant conditioning and reinforcement derived from the animal laboratory appear to apply almost without modification to some behavioral changes in the very young child or in the mentally retarded. (pp. 21-22)

And this brings me back (at last) to an earlier statement about the two directions taken by contemporary, animal-based learning theory. The second direction in which learning theory has moved (the first being toward animal cognitivism) is toward behavioral neuroscience and neuropsychology. Behavioral neuroscience, in this regard, seems, as I asserted earlier, to be more theoretically permissive than animal cognitivism; it seems more reasonably split between—and able to accommodate—the stimulus-response-associationistic and the cognitive approaches. Although many, if not most, neuroscientists have no reason to be concerned with this kind of theoretical difference, several neuropsychologists appear to un-

derstand it very well and to find it central to their work. But regardless of metatheoretical preference, unlike the cognitivist approach
to animal learning, that of the behavioral neuroscientist is generally on a two-way street: The neurophysiology/neuroanatomy is in-
tended to cast light on behavior and to influence behavior theory;
and the behavior and behavior theory are, respectively, vehicles
to examine and to attempt to comprehend the functioning of one
or another of the many systems of the brain. If we add a comparative (phylogenetic) influence and, particularly, a developmental (ontogenetic) dimension to behavior theory and a psychobiological
approach, we have a more-or-less complete description of the way
a segment of thinking, including my own, has gone in recent years.

If one studies learning and memory from an ontogenetic or from
a phylogenetic perspective, or from the perspective of brain-dam-
aged people, it should become relatively easy to accept the compromise offered some years ago (Amsel, 1972; Estes, 1975b) that
there are "lower" and "higher" levels of processing in learning
and memory and that both (or all) levels reside even in the intact
human adult, "sometimes in almost total independence, sometimes
in intricate interactions" (Estes, p. 21). Some of the best evidence,
as we shall see, is from neuropsychological investigations in humans and other primates.

Actually, this kind of idea is not a new one; it was brought into
prominence by two comparative psychologists whose points of view
were otherwise very different. In 1959, Schneirla made the important point that simple animals, both in phylogenesis and ontogen-
esis, operate on a level of *approach* and *withdrawal*, whereas more
advanced organisms operate on a level of *seeking* and *avoidance*.
In his terms, seeking and avoidance connoted expectancy or incentive, whereas approach and withdrawal had no such connotations,
but were reactions, respectively, to low and high intensity of stimulation (as in the ordinary distinction between orienting and defensive reactions)." . . . [B]oth amoeba and rat," wrote Schneirla (1959,
p. 2), "act adaptively, but only the [adult] rat accomplishes goal-
directed responses to an incentive, and therefore behaves purpo-
sively. The response of the amoeba is energized directly by pro-
toplasmic processes set off by the stimulus—that of the rat involves

specialized, higher-level processes not indicated in the protozoan."
And further, ". . . for all organisms *in early ontogenetic stages* [italics added], low intensities of stimulation tend to evoke approach
reactions [but not seeking], high intensities withdrawal [not
avoidance] reactions with reference to the source. . . . [and] the
quantitative aspects of stimulation evidently dominate both the
direction and vigor of action" (p. 3). Still further, and most meaningfully for our present purpose, "Psychologists who emphasize disproportions, reversals, and exceptions between stimulus magnitude
and response properties are therefore talking of adult stages at
higher psychological levels" (p. 22).

A year later, on the basis of a large body of cross-species experimental research, Bitterman (1960) argued, in a similar vein,
that in fishes and turtles learning does not depend on a mediating
reward expectancy (that they do not function on the basis of incentive, or on a long-term "image" or "reinstatement" of reward);
their learning depends instead on the direct stamping-in action of
a reward on an associative connection, in Thorndike's sense.

As I argued somewhat later in distinguishing among three kinds
of conditioning—"pure" classical, Pavlovian, and instrumental—
(Amsel, 1972), the simplest kinds of associative learning, habituation and pure classical conditioning, which can be seen at any level of ontogeny or phylogeny, do not at any level *require* incentives
in their formation. However, at higher levels, incentives are formed
through conditioning and serve as expectancies of reward, frustration, and punishment (Amsel, 1958), and relief (Mowrer, 1960); and
these incentives are an important aspect of the higher levels of
processing that are involved in more advanced learning. The important thing from my point of view is that incentives are necessary, though not sufficient, for detection of—and emotional reaction
to—discrepancy. Indeed, a guiding principle of our recent work (Amsel, 1986; Amsel & Stanton, 1980) is that reaction to discrepancy
is evidence of transition from one level of functioning to another.

It is interesting, and perhaps ironic, that perhaps the earliest
modern treatment of degraded human function in learning was by
Kenneth Spence and his students (Spence, 1966). He described
differences between acquisition and extinction effects in human

eyeblink conditioning with and without what he called "cognitive" involvement. He used a "cover story" and a masking procedure so that his subjects would be unaware of the fact that a light-intensity change (CS) was always (or sometimes) followed by an air puff to the eye (US). Under these conditions, extinction—the rate of decline in nonreinforced conditioned responding after both CRF and PRF training—was much slower than under normal cognitive conditions, and under these noncognitive conditions there was no PREE. Here is the normal adult human apparently operating at a level more appropriate to what I have called the "preparadoxical" infant rat.

A second example from humans of reduced levels of functioning is the difference between normal controls and certain amnesics. Korsakoff patients show normal acquisition and retention of eyeblink conditioning, but cannot recall later anything about the stimuli (CS and US) they were exposed to or their contingent relationship (Weiskrantz & Warrington, 1979). In summarizing this and other work on amnesia, Warrington and Weiskrantz (1982) refer to Spence's work, and advance the hypothesis that "the amnesic subject can show learning through facilitation by repetition of simple S-R relationships not requiring cognitive mediation" (p. 233). The famous H. M. showed good long-term memory for newly learned motor skills but no recollection of having learned the tasks (Corkin, 1968).

Another quite similar distinction has been made by Squire (1982), when he divides learning and memory into two basic levels—the procedural level (an example is simple classical conditioning), and the declarative level (more complex learning involving reaction to change, such as discrimination reversal). Squire's distinction finds support in the seminal work of R. F. Thompson and his associates (e.g., Thompson, 1983; Thompson, Berger, Berry, Hoehler, Kettner, & Weisz, 1980), who have evidence that the hippocampus is involved in, but is not necessary for, classical conditioning (which is procedural), but does seem to be necessary for more complex (declarative) learning. For the simplest kind of "reflexive" conditioning at the level of the "engram," as Thompson, following Lashley (1929), calls it, Thompson's group has identified circuitry in the cerebellum (e.g., McCormick, Lavond, Clark, Kettner, Rising, & Thompson, 1981).

Tulving (1985) has advanced a change in his thinking about his well-known distinction between two kinds of propositional memory, semantic and episodic (Tulving, 1972). He now favors a concept of "triadic memory" in which episodic and semantic memory are no longer simply parallel subsystems of declarative memory; rather, episodic memory is conceived of as "growing out of but remaining embedded in the semantic system" (p. 88), the same arrangement holding between procedural and semantic memory.

Still another distinction of the same sort has been made recently by Mishkin and others (Mishkin, Malamut, & Bachevalier, 1984; Mishkin & Petri, 1984). They refer to two different "retention systems," a habit system ("knowing how") and a memory system ("knowing that"), only the latter being impaired in most amnesias. In every one of these distinctions (and in many other similar ones) there is the at least tacit recognition of two levels of functioning, one more primary (more primitive) than the other, and therefore less dependent upon anticipation, recollection or expectancy—on confirmation and disconfirmation. One system depends on repetition and incremental associative growth; the other is less incremental and depends more on a single experience or a small number of them.

A much more explicit statement of Mishkin's recent position is contained in a brief biographical note describing his background and current interests as President of the Society for Neuroscience (*Neuroscience Newsletter*, December, 1986). It indicates that this eminent neuropsychologist is interested in

> the neural basis of learning—specifically, in the possibility that there are two distinct modes of learning that proceed simultaneously in separate neural systems. One system appears to lead to the stimulus-response connections of the behaviorists, whereas the other seems to yield the stimulus-stimulus associations of the cognitivists. If he is able to verify the existence of these two parallel learning systems [the statement continues], Dr. Mishkin' s studies could help resolve the sharp controversy that has long divided behaviorists and cognitivists in psychology. (p. 2)

I would, of course, characterize this statement as representing the positions of the neobehaviorists (not the behaviorists) and the cognitivists. In fact, it takes the specific form of the distinction first made by Spence (1951) between what is hypothesized to be learned in the theories of Hull and of Tolman: S-R associations in the case of the former, S-S relationships in the latter. Insofar as this statement about Mishkin addresses the different levels of functioning inherent in Hull's and Tolman's theorizing, the difference exists only if Hull's "Habit Strength" is compared with Tolman's "Sign-Gestalt-Expectation." The difference is greatly attenuated when one considers the functional equivalence of Hull's anticipatory-goal-response mechanism and Tolman's SGE.

To repeat, in the neuropsychological study of human memory, but, strangely, not in contemporary animal-based cognitive learning theory, the crisis necessitating a paradigmatic shift has seemed less compelling, and the associationistic and cognitive ideas have entered into explanatory partnership. All the basic distinctions that have been offered involve the different levels of functioning, though these levels go by different names: non-cognitive versus cognitive; S-R versus cognitive; procedural versus declarative; procedural versus propositional (semantic and episodic); habit systems versus memory systems. You will recall that in Schneirla's case it was approach-withdrawal versus seeking-avoidance; in Bitterman's, carryover versus reinstatement. In my own case, the levels of functioning are inherent in distinctions I have made between unmediated classical conditioning and mediated Pavlovian and instrumental conditioning (Amsel, 1972), and more recently between non-paradoxical and paradoxical functioning (Amsel, 1986).

In recent years, we (see Amsel, 1986) have examined the ontogeny of a number of reward-schedule effects, and this examination has strengthened our belief that there are indeed two systems that operate to strengthen associations and learned performance—one more "primitive" than the other. The first system involves the stamping-in action of reinforcers, which we identify with the work of Pavlov, Thorndike and the early learning theorists, and such reinforcement systems may be said to be operating in all animals, including the lower phyletic and ontogenetic forms. The second system involves the formation of incentives on the basis of the first system, and it is present perhaps in all mammals, but arguably not very early in life in the ones that are less precocious (e.g., the infant rat, the newborn human). This latter system involves expectancies related to reward, frustration, punishment and relief; it is an important aspect of the "mind" to which Hebb alluded and which he linked to motivational and emotional development. The basic flaw I see in most of cognitive psychology, and particularly in animal cognitivism, is that it does not deal with the first system: *Everything is cognitive.* As a consequence, it is unprepared to handle the conative and the affective features of the second system—the motivational and emotional determinants of behavior—which are products of the interplay of the two systems.

As an example of how learning theory can involve the two systems I have described, how it can become developmental and move toward neuroscience, some years ago these relationships between brain and behavior, in the context of development, suggested the strategy of research that is summarized in the statements that are shown in Table 2. I will close this final chapter with a brief description of how our recent work has been an attempt to follow this set of guiding principles. My purpose in this is to show how a neobehaviorist S-R theory—a theory in which mediating mechanisms are conceptualized in terms of a conditioning model—can be applied to the integration of phenomena an order of magnitude more complex than the conditioning phenomena, themselves.

As to the related behavioral effects identified as Item 1 in the table, we have in the last few years based our developmental anal-

TABLE 2

Stages in the Psychobiological Study of Related Behavioral Effects

1. Observe and describe a number of apparently related behavioral effects;
2. Develop a conceptualization of these effects in terms of empirical-construct theory;
3. Study these effects ontogenetically for their presence or absence at various developmental stages, and for the order of their first appearance;
4. Study these effects for their presence or absence in relation to the presence or absence of portions of, or activities of, their presumed neural substrate;
5. Relate the order of appearance of the effects to the developing neural substrate;
6. Modify empirical-construct theory on the basis of findings from 4 and 5.

ysis of the reward/frustration system on a family of reward-schedule phenomena. These behavioral effects are seen in all mammalian species that have been studied, including humans. Item 2 refers to our conceptualization of the more advanced of these effects, the paradoxical ones, which has been in terms of frustrative reactions to inconsistency or discrepancy, and of conditioned forms of these reactions as mediators. This is the level of functioning that Schneirla referred to as "seeking and avoidance." Of course there have been other attempts at theoretical integration of some of these effects, the major one being Capaldi's (1967).[3] Referring to Item 3, we have been able to identify the ages of first appearance in ontogeny of these effects. These are listed in Table 3. We have thought of this ontogenetic sequence as representing successive developmental levels of associative processing and of temperamental-emotional functioning. We think of the first two effects (the earliest appearing ones) as being at Schneirla's more primitive level of approach and withdrawal. Going back to Table 2, and referring to Item 4, it is the case that in adult rats some of these effects have been shown to depend upon the integrity of the hippocampal formation, including its connections to septum and entorhinal cortex. As to Item 5, portions of this neuroanatomical system show a rapid rate of development in the age-range (about 10-25 days) of our developing reward-schedule effects.

And, finally (Item 6), what we have been able to show is that the order of first appearance in ontogeny of these effects—along with some of our correlated work with infant hippocampal lesions and fetal alcohol effects—does not entirely conform to our theoretical treatments of them based on adult behavior. Our conclusion

---

[3]An interesting point: Despite the fact that Amsel's theorizing involves the concepts of anticipation (expectancy) and mediation, and Capaldi's work was based initially on direct unmediated S-R association in the Hull-Sheffield (Sheffield, 1949) mode of explanation, the animal cognitivists find the latter more kindred to their position than the former, perhaps for two reasons. First, Capaldi's later work refers to short-term memories and much of the cognitivist work is a "working memory" kind of approach to cognition, not a long-term memory approach. Since Capaldi's major contribution has been to working memory, it could readily revert to its S-R origins, with no loss, and probably a gain, in precision. Second, Capaldi's elegant theorizing is purely associative, and involves no obvious motivational constructs; and motivational explanation is not a feature of cognitive theorizing.

TABLE 3
Age of First Appearance of Various Reinforcement-Schedule Effects

Effect	Age
Successive Acquisition and Extinction	–10 Days
Single Patterned Alternation (PA)	–11 Days
Partial Reinforcement Extinction (PREE)	12–14 Days
Variable Magnitude of Reinforcement (VMREE)	16–18 Days
Partial Delay of Reinforcement (PDREE)	16–18 Days
Partial Reinforcement Acquisition (PRAE)	18–20 Days
Magnitude Reinforcement Extinction (MREE)	20–21 Days
Successive Negative Contrast	25–26 Days
Slow Responding (DNC)	21–63 Days

has been that these developmental and neurobehavioral data point to a modification of a theory of frustration, suppression and persistence with which I have been associated for about 30 years (Amsel, 1986).

I have presented this little closing vignette of our work to show how a simple neobehavioristic conditioning model can lead to the integration of a number of more complex behavioral processes, to considerations of development and even neurobiology, and to a modification or even to a possible disconfirmation of the model with which it all began. Among the difficulties inherent in animal models based on pure cognitivism, as I see them, one is that such models postulate representational processes even at the lowest ontogenetic and phylogenetic levels. This being the case, these models would not lead their supporters to look for evidence from behavioral development, or from developmental neuroanatomy and neurophysiology; nor would these cognitive models lead their advocates to examine or even consider transitions from one level of functioning to another—or to consider the simultaneous existence of both levels.

Finally, in models based on animal cognitivism, as in cognitive theories in general, there appear at times to be as many models as there are experimental phenomena; and disconfirmation, if it is possible in principle, is difficult to come by in practice. And, as so many philosophers of science agree, disconfirmation is "the only game in town."

References

Alkon, D. L. (1974). Associative training of *Hermissenda*. *Journal of General Physiology, 64,* 70–84.

Amsel, A. (1949). Selective association and the anticipatory goal response mechanism as explanatory concepts in learning theory. *Journal of Experimental Psychology, 39,* 785–799.

Amsel, A. (1950). The combination of a primary appetitional need with primary and secondary emotionally derived needs. *Journal of Experimental Psychology, 40,* 1–14.

Amsel, A. (1958). The role of frustrative nonreward in noncontinuous reward situations. *Psychological Bulletin, 55,* 102–119.

Amsel, A. (1961). Hope comes to learning theory. [Review of O. H. Mowrer's *Learning theory and behavior*.] *Contemporary Psychology, 6,* 33–36.

Amsel, A. (1962). Frustrative nonreward in partial reinforcement and discrimination learning: Some recent history and a theoretical extension. *Psychological Review, 69,* 306–328.

Amsel, A. (1965). On inductive versus deductive approaches and neo-Hullian behaviorism. In B. B. Wolman & E. Nagel (Eds.), *Scientific psychology: Principles and approaches.* New York: Basic Books.

Amsel, A. (1967). Partial reinforcement effects on vigor and persistence: Advances in frustration theory derived from a variety of within-subjects experiments. In K. W. Spence & J. T. Spence (Eds.), *The psychology of learning and motivation: Advances in research and theory* (Vol. 1). New York: Academic Press.

Amsel, A. (1971). Frustration, persistence, and regression. In H. D. Kimmel (Ed.), *Experimental psychopathology: Recent research and theory.* New York: Academic Press.

Amsel, A. (1972). Inhibition and mediation in classical, Pavlovian and instrumental conditioning. In R. Boakes and S. Halliday (Eds.), *Inhibition and learning.* London: Academic Press.

Amsel, A. (1982). Behaviorism then and now [A retrospective review of J. B. Watson's *Psychology from the standpoint of a behaviorist*]. *Contemporary Psychology, 27,* 343–346.

Amsel, A. (1986). Developmental psychobiology and behavior theory: Reciprocating influences [Daniel E. Berlyne Memorial lecture]. *Canadian Journal of Psychology, 40,* 311–342.

Amsel, A., & Maltzman, I. (1950). The effect upon generalized drive strength of emotionality as inferred from the level of consummatory response. *Journal of Experimental Psychology, 40,* 563–569.

Amsel, A., & Rashotte, M. E. (1977). Entwicklungsrichtungen der S-R-Lerntheorien in Amerika: Mit spezieller Berücksichtigung Clark L. Hulls, seiner Vorgänger und Nachfolger [A perspective on S-R learning theory in America with particular reference to Clark L. Hull, his precursors and followers]. In H. Zeier (Ed.), *Die Psychologie des 20. Jarhunderts: Vol. 4. Pawlow und die Folgern.* Zurich: Kindler.

Amsel, A., & Rashotte, M. E. (1984). *Mechanisms of adaptive behavior: Clark L. Hull's theoretical papers, with commentary.* New York: Columbia University Press.

Amsel, A., & Stanton, M. (1980). Ontogeny and phylogeny of paradoxical reward effects. In J. S. Rosenblatt, R. A. Hinde, C. Beer, & M. Busnel (Eds.), *Advances in the study of behavior.* New York: Academic Press.

Amsel, A., & Ward, J. S. (1965). Frustration and persistence: Resistance to discrimination following prior experience with the discriminanda. *Psychological Monographs, 79,* (4, Whole No. 597).

Bergmann, G. (1956). The contribution of John B. Watson. *Psychological Review, 63,* 265–276.

Bitterman, M. E. (1960). Towards a comparative psychology of learning. *American Psychologist, 15,* 704–712

Bitterman, M. E. (1975). The comparative analysis of learning. *Science, 188,* 699–709.

Bitterman, M. E. (1976). Flavor aversion studies. *Science, 192,* 266–267.

Bolles, R. C. (1975). Learning, motivation, and cognition. In W. K. Estes (Ed.), *Handbook of learning and cognitive processes: Volume 1. Introduction to concepts and issues.* Hillsdale, NJ: Lawrence Erlbaum Associates.

Bower, G. H. (1975). Cognitive psychology: An introduction. In W. K. Estes (Ed.), *Handbook of learning and cognitive processes: Volume 1. Introduction to concepts and issues.* Hillsdale, NJ: Lawrence Erlbaum Associates.

Bower, G. H. (1981). Mood and memory. *American Psychologist, 36,* 129–148.

Bridgman, P. W. (1927). *The logic of modern physics.* New York: Macmillan.

Brown, J. S., & Farber, I. E. (1951). Emotions conceptualized as intervening variables—with suggestions toward a theory of frustration. *Psychological Bulletin, 48,* 465–495.

Burghardt, G. M. (1985). Animal awareness: Current perceptions and historical perspective. *American Psychologist, 40,* 905–919.

Bush, R. R., & Mosteller, F. (1951). A mathematical model for simple learning. *Psychological Review, 58,* 313–323.

Capaldi, E. J. (1967). A sequential hypothesis of instrumental learning. In. K. W. Spence & J. T. Spence (Eds.), *The psychology of learning and motivation* (Vol. 1). New York: Academic Press.

Carew, T. J., Abrams, T. W., Hawkins, R. D., & Kandel, E. R. (1984). The use of simple invertebrate systems to explore psychological issues related to associative learning. In D. L. Alkon & J. Farley (Eds.), *Primary neural substrates of learning and behavioral change.* New York: Cambridge University Press.

Chomsky, N. (1959). [A review of B. F. Skinner's *Verbal Behavior*]. *Language, 35,* 26–58.

Corkin, S. (1968). Acquisition of motor skill after bilateral temporal lobe excisions. *Neuropsychologia, 6,* 225–265.

Denny, M. R. (1986). "Retention" of S-R in the midst of the cognitive invasion. In D. F. Kendrick, M. E. Rilling, & M. R. Denny (Eds.), *Theories of animal memory.* Hillsdale, NJ: Lawrence Erlbaum Associates.

Dickinson, A. (1979). [Review of *Cognitive processes in animal behavior.*] *Quarterly Journal of Experimental Psychology, 31,* 551–554.

Dickinson, A. (1980). *Contemporary animal learning theory.* New York: Cambridge University Press.

Dinsmoor, J. A. (1983). Observing and conditioned reinforcement. *Behavioral and Brain Sciences, 6,* 693–728.

Dollard, J. & Miller, N. E. (1950). *Personality and psychotherapy.* New York: McGraw-Hill.

Estes, W. K. (1950). Toward a statistical theory of learning. *Psychological Review, 57,* 94–107.

Estes, W. K. (1958). Stimulus-response theory of drive. In M. R. Jones (Ed.), *Nebraska Symposium on Motivation* (Vol. 6). Lincoln, NE: University of Nebraska Press.

Estes, W. K. (1975a). *Handbook of learning and cognitive processes: Volume 1. Introduction to concepts and methods.* Hillsdale, NJ: Lawrence Erlbaum Associates.

Estes, W. K. (1975b). The state of the field: General problems and issues of theory and metatheory. In W. K. Estes (Ed.), *Handbook of learning and cognitive processes: Volume 1. Introduction to concepts and issues.* Hillsdale, NJ: Lawrence Erlbaum Associates.

Estes, W. K., & Skinner, B. F. (1941). Some quantitative properties of anxiety. *Journal of Experimental Psychology, 29,* 390–400.

Feldman, J. A., & Ballard, D. H. (1982). Connectionist models and their properties. *Cognitive Science, 6,* 205–254.

Feuer, L. S. (1974). *Einstein and the generations of science.* New York: Basic Books

Fodor, J. A. (1986). Why paramecia don't have mental representations. *Midwest Studies in Philosophy, 10,* 3–24.

Garcia, J., Hankins, W. G., & Rusiniak, K. W. (1976). Flavor aversion studies. *Science, 192,* 265–266.

Garcia, J., & Koelling, R. A. (1966). Relation of cue to consequence in avoidance learning. *Psychonomic Science, 4,* 123–124.

Griffin, D. R. (1976) *The question of animal awareness.* New York: Rockefeller University Press.

Guthrie, E. R. (1935). *The psychology of learning.* New York: Harper.

Hawkins, R. D., & Kandel, E. R. (1984). Is there a cell-biological alphabet for simple forms of learning? *Psychological Review, 91,* 375–391.

Hebb, D. O. (1949). *The organization of behavior.* New York: Wiley.

Hebb, D. O. (1955). Drives and the CNS (conceptual nervous system). *Psychological Review, 62,* 243–254.

Hebb, D. O. (1980). *Essays on mind.* Hillsdale, NJ: Lawrence Erlbaum Associates.

Hennessey, T. M., Rucker, W. B., & McDiarmid, C. G. (1979). Classical conditioning in paramecia. *Animal Learning & Behavior, 7,* 417–423.

Herrnstein, R. J., & DeVilliers, P. A. (1980). Fish as a natural category for people and pigeons. In G. H. Bower (Ed.), *The psychology of learning and motivation* (Vol. 14). New York: Academic Press.

Herrnstein, R. J., Loveland, D. H., & Cable, C. (1976). Natural concepts in pigeons. *Journal of Experimental Psychology: Animal Behavior Processes, 2,* 285–302.

Honig, W. K. (1978). Studies of working memory in the pigeon. In S. H. Hulse, D. Fowler, & W. K. Honig (Eds.), *Cognitive processes in animal behavior.* Hillsdale, NJ: Lawrence Erlbaum Associates.

Hubel, D. H., & Wiesel, T. N. (1962). Receptive fields, binocular interaction and functional architecture in the cat's visual cortex. *Journal of Physiology, 160,* 106–154.

Hull, C. L. (1930). Knowledge and purpose as habit mechanisms. *Psychological Review, 37,* 511–525.

Hull, C. L. (1931). Goal attraction and directing ideas conceived as habit phenomena. *Psychological Review, 38,* 487–506.

Hull, C. L. (1934). The concept of the habit-family hierarchy and maze learning: Part 1. *Psychological Review, 41,* 33–54. (See also Part 2. *Psychological Review, 41,* 134–152.)

Hull, C. L. (1935). The mechanism of the assembly of behavior segments in novel combinations suitable for problem solution. *Psychological Review, 42,* 219–245.

Hull, C. L. (1937). Mind, mechanism, and adaptive behavior. *Psychological Review, 44,* 1–32.

Hull, C. L. (1943). *Principles of behavior.* New York: Appleton-Century-Crofts.

Hull, C. L. (1952). *A behavior system.* New Haven: Yale University Press.

Hull, C. L., Hovland, C. I., Ross, R. T., Hall, M., Perkins, D. T., & Fitch, F. B. (1940). *Mathematico-deductive theory of rote learning.* New Haven: Yale University Press.

Hulse, S. H., Fowler, H., & Honig, W. K. (1978). *Cognitive processes in animal behavior.* Hillsdale, NJ: Lawrence Erlbaum Associates.

Jacob, F. (1977). Evolution and tinkering. *Science, 196,* 1161–1166.

Kamin, L. J. (1968). "Attention-like" processes in classical conditioning. In M. R. Jones (Ed.), *Miami symposium on the prediction of behavior: Aversive stimulation.* Miami, FL: University of Miami Press.

Kamin, L. J. (1969). Predictability, surprise, attention and conditioning. In B. A. Campbell & R. M. Church (Eds.), *Punishment and aversive behavior.* New York: Appleton-Century-Crofts.

Kendler, H. H. (1946). The influence of simultaneous hunger and thirst drives upon the learning of two opposed spatial responses in the white rat. *Journal of Experimental Psychology, 36,* 212–220.

Kendler, H. H. (1985). Behaviorism and psychology: An uneasy alliance. In S. Koch & D. E. Leary (Eds.), *A century of psychology as science.* New York: McGraw-Hill.

Kendler, H. H. (1987). *Historical foundations of modern psychology.* Chicago: Dorsey Press.

Kendler, T. S. (1971). Continuity theory and cue-dominance. In H. H. Kendler & J. T. Spence (Eds.), *Essays in neobehaviorism: A memorial volume to Kenneth W. Spence.* New York: Appleton-Century-Crofts.

Kihlstrom, J. F. (1987). The cognitive unconscious. *Science, 237,* 1445–1452.

Killeen, P. R. (1987). Emergent behaviorism. In S. Mogdil & C. Mogdil (Eds.), *B. F. Skinner: Consensus and controversy.* London: Falmer.

Kimble, G. A. (1961). *Hilgard and Marquis' conditioning and learning.* New York: Appleton-Century-Crofts.

Koestler, A. (1964). *The act of creation.* New York: Macmillan.

Konorski, J. (1967). *Integrative activity of the brain.* Chicago: University of Chicago Press.

Krechevsky, I. (1938). A study of the continuity of the problem-solving process. *Psychological Review, 45,* 107–133.

Kuhn, T. S. (1962). *The structure of scientific revolutions.* Chicago: University of Chicago Press.

Lashley, K. S. (1929). *Brain mechanisms and intelligence.* Chicago: University of Chicago Press.

Levin, H. (1987). Successions in psychology. [Review of *The Cognitive Revolution in Psychology*]. *Science, 236,* 1683–1684.

Lewin, K. (1987). Do animals read minds, tell lies? *Science, 238,* 1350–1351.

Lloyd, D. (1986). The limits of cognitive liberalism. *Behaviorism, 14,* 1–14.

Mandler, G. (1979). Emotion. In E. Hearst (Ed.), *The first century of experimental psychology.* Hillsdale, NJ: Lawrence Erlbaum Associates.

Mandler, G. (1984). *Mind and body: Psychology of emotion and stress.* New York: Norton.

Marr, J. (1983). Memory: Model and metaphors. *Psychological Record, 33,* 12–19.

McCormick, D. A., Lavond, D. G., Clark, G. A., Kettner, R. E., Rising, C. E., & Thompson, R. F. (1981). The engram found? Role of the cerebellum in classical conditioning of nictitating membrane and eyelid responses. *Bulletin of the Psychonomic Society, 18,* 103–105.

Miller, G. A. (1962). Some psychological studies of grammar. *American Psychologist, 17,* 748–762.

Miller, G. A., Galanter, E., & Pribram, K. H. (1960). *Plans and the structure of behavior.* New York: Holt.

Miller, N. E. (1935). A reply to "Sign-Gestalt or conditioned reflex?" *Psychological Review, 42,* 280–292.

Miller, N. E. (1944). Experimental studies of conflict. In J. McV. Hunt (Ed.), *Personality and the behavior disorders: Vol. 1.* New York: Ronald.

Miller, N. E. (1959). Liberalization of basic S-R concepts: Extensions to conflict behavior, motivation, and social learning. In S. Koch (Ed.), *Psychology: A study of a science* (Vol. 2). New York: McGraw-Hill.

Mishkin, M., Malamut, B., & Bachevalier, J. (1984). Memories and habits: Two neural systems. In G. Lynch, J. L. McGaugh, & N. M. Weinberger (Eds.), *Neurobiology of learning and memory.* New York: Guilford.

Mishkin, M., & Petri, H. L. (1984). Memories and habits: Some implications for the analysis of learning and retention. In L. R. Squire & N. Butters (Eds.), *Neuropsychology of memory.* New York: Guilford.

Moore, J. (1983). Symposium proceedings: Introductory remarks. *Psychological Record, 33,* 3–6.

Morruzi, G., & Magoun, H. W. (1949). Brain stem reticular formation and activation of the EEG. *Electroencephalography and Clinical Neurophysiology, 1,* 455–473.

Mowrer, O. H. (1939). A stimulus-response analysis of anxiety and its role as a reinforcing agent. *Psychological Review, 46,* 553–565.

Mowrer, O. H. (1960). *Learning theory and behavior.* New York: Wiley.

Mowrer, O. H., & Lamoreaux, R. R. (1946). Fear as an intervening variable in avoidance conditioning. *Journal of Comparative Psychology, 39,* 29–50.

Neisser, U. (1967). *Cognitive psychology.* New York: Appleton-Century-Crofts.

Pearce, J. M. (1987). *An introduction to animal cognition.* Hove and London: Lawrence Erlbaum Associates.

Pratt, C. C. (1939). *The logic of modern psychology.* New York: Macmillan.

Rashotte, M. E., & Amsel, A. (1968). Transfer of slow-response rituals to the extinction of a continuously rewarded response. *Journal of Comparative and Physiological Psychology, 66,* 432–443.

Rescorla, R. A. (1967). Pavlovian conditioning and its proper control procedures. *Psychological Review, 74,* 71–80.

Rescorla, R. A. (1969). Pavlovian conditioned inhibition. *Psychological Bulletin, 72,* 77–94.

Rescorla, R. A. (1972). Informational variables in Pavlovian conditioning. In G. H. Bower (Ed.), *The psychology of learning and motivation* (Vol. 6). New York: Academic Press.

Rescorla, R. A. (1978). Some implications of a cognitive perspective in Pavlovian conditioning. In S. H. Hulse, H. Fowler, & W. K. Honig (Eds.), *Cognitive processes in animal behavior.* Hillsdale, NJ: Lawrence Erlbaum Associates.

Rescorla, R. A. (1980). *Pavlovian second-order conditioning: Studies in associative learning.* Hillsdale, NJ: Lawrence Erlbaum Associates.

Rescorla, R. A. (1985). Conditioned inhibition and facilitation. In R. R. Miller & N. E. Spear (Eds.), *Information processing in animals: Conditioned inhibition.* Hillsdale, NJ: Lawrence Erlbaum Associates.

Rescorla, R. A., & Wagner, A. R. (1972). A theory of Pavlovian conditioning: Variations in the effectiveness of reinforcement and nonreinforcement. In A. H. Black and W. F. Prokasy (Eds.), *Classical conditioning II: Current theory and research.* New York: Appleton-Century-Crofts.

Rogers, C. R. (1964). Toward a science of the person. In W. T. Wann (Ed.), *Behaviorism and phenomenology.* Chicago: University of Chicago Press.

Roitblat, H. L., Bever, T. G., & Terrace, H. S. (1984). *Animal cognition.* Hillsdale, NJ: Lawrence Erlbaum Associates.

Ross, R. R. (1964). Positive and negative partial-reinforcement extinction effects carried through continuous reinforcement, changed motivation, and changed response. *Journal of Experimental Psychology, 68,* 492–502.

Rozeboom, W. W. (1970). The art of metascience, or, what should a psychological theory be? In J. R. Royce (Ed.), *Toward unification in psychology.* Toronto, Ontario: University of Toronto Press.

Schachter, S., & Singer, J. E. (1962). Cognitive, social, and physiological determinants of emotional state. *Psychological Review, 69,* 379–399.

Schneirla, T. C. (1959). An evolutionary and developmental theory of biphasic processes underlying approach and withdrawal. In M. R. Jones (Ed.), *Nebraska symposium on motivation.* Lincoln, NE: University of Nebraska Press.

Schwartz, B., & Lacey, H. (1982). *Behaviorism, science, and human nature.* New York: Norton.

Shannon, C. E., & Weaver, W. (1949). *The mathematical theory of communication.* Urbana, IL: University of Illinois Press.

Sheffield, V. F. (1949). Extinction as a function of partial reinforcement and distribution of practice. *Journal of Experimental Psychology, 39,* 511–526.

Shimp, C. P. (1976). Short-term memory in the pigeon: The previously reinforced response. *Journal of the Experimental Analysis of Behavior, 26,* 487–493.

Shimp, C. P. (1982). Metaknowledge in the pigeon: An organism's knowledge about its own adaptive behavior. *Animal Learning & Behavior, 10,* 358–364.

Shimp, C. P. (1983). The local organization of behavior: A dissociation between a pigeon's behavior and a self-report of that behavior. *Journal of the Experimental Analysis of Behavior, 39,* 61–68.

Siegel, P. S., & Brantley, J. J. (1951). The relationship of emotionality to the consummatory response of eating. *Journal of Experimental Psychology, 42,* 304–306.

Siegel, P. S., & Siegel, H. S. (1949). The effect of emotionality on the water intake of the rat. *Journal of Comparative and Physiological Psychology, 42,* 12–16.

Simon, H. A. (1967). Motivational and emotional controls of cognition. *Psychological Review, 74,* 29–39.

Simon, H. A. (1980). The behavioral and social sciences. *Science, 209,* 72–78.

Simonov, P. V. (1969). Studies of emotional behavior of humans and animals by Soviet physiologists. *Annals of the New York Academy of Science, 159,* 1112–1121.

Skinner, B. F. (1938). *The behavior of organisms.* New York: Appleton-Century-Crofts.

Skinner, B. F. (1950). Are theories of learning necessary? *Psychological Review, 57,* 193–216.

Skinner, B. F. (1957). *Verbal behavior.* New York: Appleton-Century-Crofts.

Skinner, B. F. (1959). John Broadus Watson, behaviorist. *Science, 129,* 197–198.

Skinner, B. F. (1966). The phylogeny and ontogeny of behavior. *Science, 150,* 1205–1213.

Skinner, B. F. (1977). Why I am not a cognitive psychologist. *Behaviorism, 5,* 1–10.

Skinner, B. F. (1987a, May 8). Outlining a science of feeling. *Times Literary Supplement,* pp. 1–5.

Skinner, B. F. (1987b). *Origins of cognitive thought.* Paper presented at the convention of the American Psychological Association, New York.

Spence, K. W. (1937). The differential response in animals to stimuli varying within a single dimension. *Psychological Review, 44,* 430–444.

Spence, K. W. (1940). Continuous versus non-continuous interpretations of discrimination learning. *Psychological Review, 47,* 271–288.

Spence, K. W. (1951). Theoretical interpretations of learning. In C. P. Stone (Ed.), *Comparative Psychology.* Englewood Cliffs, NJ: Prentice-Hall.

Spence, K. W. (1966). Cognitive and drive factors in the extinction of the conditioned eye-blink in human subjects. *Psychological Review, 73,* 445–458.

Squire, L. R. (1982). The neuropsychology of human memory. *Annual Reviews of Neuroscience, 5,* 241–273.

Terrace, H. S. (1984). Animal cognition. In H. L. Roitblat, T. G. Bever, & H. S. Terrace (Eds.), *Animal cognition.* Hillsdale, NJ: Lawrence Erlbaum Associates.

Thompson, R. F. (1983). Neuronal substrate of simple associative learning: Classical conditioning. *Trends in Neuroscience, 6,* 270–272.

Thompson, R. F., Berger, T. W., Berry, S. D., Hoehler, F. K., Kettner, R. E., & Weisz, D. J. (1980). Hippocampal substrate of classical conditioning. *Physiological Psychology, 8,* 262–279.

Thurstone, L. L. (1919). The learning curve equation. *Psychological Monographs, 26* (Whole No. 114).

Titchener, E. B. (1910). *A text-book of psychology.* New York: MacMillan.

Tolman, E. C. (1932). *Purposive behavior in animals and men.* Berkeley, CA: University of California Press.

Tolman, E. C. (1938). The determination of behavior at a choice point. *Psychological Review, 45,* 1–41.

Tolman, E. C. (1948). Cognitive maps in rats and men. *Psychological Review, 53,* 189–208.

Tulving, E. (1972). Episodic and semantic memory. In E. Tulving & W. Donaldson (Eds.), *Organization of Memory.* New York: Academic Press.

Tulving, E. (1985). On the classification problem in learning and memory. In L. G. Nilsson & T. Archer (Eds.), *Perspectives on learning and memory.* Hillsdale, NJ: Lawrence Erlbaum Associates.

Wagner, A. R. (1976). Priming in STM: An information processing mechanism for self-generated or retrieval-generated depression in performance. In T. J. Tighe & R. N. Leaton (Eds.), *Habituation: Perspectives from child development, animal behavior, and neurophysiology.* Hillsdale, NJ: Lawrence Erlbaum Associates.

Wagner, A. R. (1978). Expectancies and the priming of STM. In S. H. Hulse, H. Fowler, & W. K. Honig (Eds.), *Cognitive processes in animal behavior.* Hillsdale, NJ: Lawrence Erlbaum Associates.

Warrington, E. K., & Weiskrantz, L. (1982). Amnesia: A disconnection syndrome. *Neuropsychologia, 20,* 233–248.

Watson, J. B. (1913). Psychology as the behaviorist views it. *Psychological Review, 20,* 158–177.

Watson, J. B. (1914). *Behavior: An introduction to comparative psychology.* New York: Holt.

Watson, J. B. (1916). The place of the conditioned reflex in psychology. *Psychological Review, 23,* 89–116.

Watson, J. B. (1919). *Psychology from the standpoint of a behaviorists.* Philadelphia: Lippincott.

Watson, J. B. (1930). *Behaviorism* (rev. ed.). New York: Norton. (Original work published 1925.)

Watson, J. B., & Rayner, R. (1920). Conditioned emotional reactions. *Journal of Experimental Psychology, 3,* 1–14.

Weiskrantz, L., & Warrington, E. K. (1979). Conditioning in amnesic patients. *Neuropsychologia, 17,* 187–194.

Zentall, T. R., & Hogan, D. E. (1976). Pigeons can learn identity, or difference, or both. *Science, 191,* 408–409.

Zuriff, G. E. (1976). Stimulus equivalence, grammar, and internal structure. *Behaviorism, 4,* 43–52.

Author Index

99

Subject Index